Literacy and Your Deaf Child

Literacy and Your Deaf Child

What Every Parent Should Know

David A. Stewart and
Bryan R. Clarke

Gallaudet University Press
Washington, D.C.

http://gupress.gallaudet.edu

Library of Congress Cataloging-in-Publication Data

Stewart, David Alan, 1954–
    Literacy and your deaf child: what every parent should know / David A. Stewart and Bryan R. Clarke.
        p. cm.
    Includes bibliographical references and index.
    ISBN 1-56368-136-6 (alk. paper)
        1. Deaf children–Education. 2. Deaf children–Language. 3. Language acquisition–Parent participation. 4. Literacy. I. Clarke, Bryan R. II. Title.

HV2465 .S735 2003
371.91′2–dc21
                                                                    2002192514

⊗ The paper used in this publication meets the minimum requirements of American National Standard for Information Sciences—Permanence of Paper for Printed Library Materials, ANSI Z39.48–1984.

CONTENTS

PREFACE

This book is for parents seeking to help their deaf child become a proficient reader and writer and develop overall literacy skills that will enable him to function in an increasingly print-oriented world. The two major goals are

1. To provide parents with background information so that they might better understand the relationship of language to reading and writing, the terminology commonly associated with discussions about literacy, the challenges that deaf children face when learning to read and write, and the role of schools in teaching literacy
2. To suggest activities that parents can do at home that will help their deaf child become literate

The basic premise of this book is that the acquisition of proficient literacy skills is the most important educational task facing deaf children. These skills are the enabling factors that allow deaf children to access the curriculum, seek information from the Internet and use e-mail correspondence, socialize with friends using TTYs and on-line conversations, attain a postsecondary education, and more generally prepare for a lifestyle that benefits greatly from the ability to read and write.

Chapter 1 introduces some common concepts associated with literacy and provides a rationale for parental involvement in their deaf child's education. Chapter 2 provides an outline of how children acquire language. Chapters 3 and 4 are concerned with the auditory and visual links to literacy so that parents can make more informed decisions regarding hearing aids, cochlear implants, speechreading, and signed communication, all of which can have a marked influence on their child's language development. Chapters 5 and 6 explain how parents can facilitate literacy development in their deaf child around the home and in the community. Chapters 7 and 8 talk about the development of reading and writing skills and provide suggestions for facilitating the development of these skills. Chapter 9 examines the way parents can work with schools and teachers to improve their child's learning environment. Chapter 9 also reinforces the key points made throughout this book with respect to the responsibilities parents can accept in helping their deaf child on his journey to literacy.

The term *deaf children* is used throughout this book to refer to both deaf and hard of hearing individuals. The use of a single term helps overcome the awkwardness of using the phrase "deaf and hard of hearing children." We are following the convention of using a lower case *d* in the word *deaf* when it is used in its audiological sense to refer to people with a hearing loss. We use the upper case *D* in *Deaf* when it is used in a sociological sense to refer to people with some degree of hearing loss, who use sign language, and have an affiliation with the Deaf community.

In the absence of a third-person-singular pronoun that refers to both genders, we have elected to use the pronoun *he* to refer to a child and *she* as a referent for the caregiver, parent, and teacher. This does not imply that females are superior to males (or vice versa) or that males cannot be caregivers, parents, or teachers. No sexual bias is intended: The choice is simply a stylistic convention adopted to avoid the clumsy and confusing use of *they* and the impersonal, if not offensive, use of *it*.

Throughout this book, we are mainly concerned with English and, to a lesser extent, with American Sign Language (ASL). This book is about how parents can help their deaf children acquire literacy skills, which, in their simplest form, are the abilities to read and write. However, ASL does have a critical role in the literacy development of those deaf children who use signed communication, and we recognize this with discussions throughout the book about the linkage between ASL and literacy.

Literacy and Your Deaf Child

CHAPTER 1

What's All This Talk about Literacy?

This chapter will help you understand

- The importance of literacy in the lives of deaf children
- The role that the family has in promoting literacy at home
- The challenges faced by deaf children learning to read and write

---

Reading and writing have always been important in the lives of deaf people. These skills help them use ATMs and read fast food menus, surf the Internet and skim newspapers, talk on TTYs and chat on-line, and watch captioned TV. Their livelihood is dependent upon their ability to read and write, and the computer age is accelerating this dependency. Although the impact of being able to read and write is different from one person to the next, we do know that being illiterate is, at best, a ticket to a low-paying job and quite possibly a life reliant on government social security and other organizations for assistance.

Schools, too, are wrapped up in the importance of the printed word, and literacy is the hottest topic of discussion in the education of deaf children. It permeates every nook and cranny of every classroom where there is a deaf child. It is the cornerstone of most programs, irrespective of school setting and method of communication, and teachers in both signing and oral programs extol the benefits of becoming literate. Today, it would appear

1

that literacy even transcends discussions about whether a child should use American Sign Language (ASL) or English signs, wear hearing aids or a cochlear implant, attend a school for deaf children or be fully integrated into a public school system, aim for a career as a laborer or prepare for university. It makes no difference whether a deaf child has Deaf parents or hearing parents or whether they are in an inner city, rural, or affluent suburban school district; every school and every teacher want deaf children to master the English language, with print as the primary medium for doing so.

The emphasis on literacy is nothing new in the field of deaf education. Deaf children were taught to read and write when Laurent Clerc and Thomas Gallaudet opened the first school for deaf children in the United States back in 1817, and teaching techniques relating to reading and writing have always been a staple in teacher training programs.

Yet, the average deaf child is leaving school with a reading level that hovers around the fourth-grade level. Because of this low achievement standard, some might argue that it is time to shift the primary focus of education away from reading and writing practices to some other aspect of learning. We counter this suggestion with the argument that teaching reading and writing is not the same as teaching literacy.

In fact, teachers and parents have to realize that the ability to decode and encode words is but one aspect of becoming literate. If all that schools do is help deaf children acquire the ability to recognize and write out words on a page, then the low reading levels of our deaf high school graduates should come as no surprise.

Parents, too, need to realize that their role in helping deaf children develop strong literacy skills extends far beyond reading a book to a child, imposing a time for reading at home, and explaining the meaning of the occasional word in print. Our goal is to help you as a parent create a positive and stimulating literacy-rich atmosphere at home that encourages your deaf child to willingly engage in the process of learning to read and write.

What Is Literacy?

Long before they even thought of reading and writing, our earliest ancestors lived in an unkind environment where they had to struggle hard to survive. In order for values, customs, beliefs, and traditions to be passed on, they needed to create a language of signs and sounds. More than likely those skills necessary for survival such as building shelter, gathering food, and making tools or weapons were handed down from generation to generation through the use of an invented language. Much later, symbols, pictographs, and eventually letters would represent these spoken or signed concepts. Written language had arrived, and man had truly taken a giant step forward into literacy. However, centuries would pass before listening and speaking or watching and signing would be complemented by reading and writing.

The term *literate* was first used in more modern times to designate an erudite or learned person who could read and write. Then later still, literacy came to be regarded as an all or none affair—a person was either literate or illiterate. In schools, the dividing line was some arbitrary level such as a grade or age score on a reading test or the number of completed years of schooling. At various times in our history, these or similar benchmarks were used to count the number of illiterates with a view to eradicating illiteracy. However, in recent years, literacy has been regarded as a continuum, and emphasis has shifted to the improvement of literacy skills rather than the elimination of illiteracy. This movement to improve levels of literacy has received very strong support from a variety of sources. Economists, for example, maintain that high levels of literacy are crucial to a nation's economic growth and development, and further grist to the mill has been added by social scientists who consider literacy as the major predictor of social cohesion.

Defining Literacy

For many people, literacy means the ability to communicate, to read and write, to calculate and, with the advent of cyberspace, use a computer. The latter is made evident by the recently invented term *computer-literate*. A more comprehensive definition, however, has been put forth by the twelve countries participating in the International Adult Literacy Survey (IALS), which has carried out several cross-national comparisons (National Center for Educational Statistics 1998). It regarded literacy as the

> ability to understand and employ printed information in daily activities at home, at work and in the community—to achieve one's goals and to develop one's knowledge and potential.

In other words, literacy is about how we use print to carry out various functions in our lives. Although literacy implies the ability to read and write, it also requires a host of other skills, such as knowledge of the social conventions of communication, awareness of the subject about which one is writing, and the ability to predict how someone might react to one's writing.

The National Institute on Literacy typically used the following three domains to measure how well a person can process printed information:

1. Prose literacy. The knowledge and skills needed to understand and use information from various texts, including editorials, news, stories, poems, and fiction.
2. Document literacy. The knowledge and skills required to locate and use information contained in various formats, including job applications, payroll forms, transportation schedules, maps, tables, and graphs.
3. Quantitative literacy. The knowledge and skills required to apply arithmetic operations either alone or sequentially to numbers embedded in printed materials, such as balancing a checkbook, figuring out a tip, completing an order form, or determining the amount of interest on a loan from an advertisement.

The participants' performance in each domain is recorded as a score (based on a scale from 0 to 500), and the results are divided into five levels starting at the lowest end. From these levels, we can then make some decisions about the literacy skills of a group of people (see box titled "Fast Facts on Literacy").

According to the National Adult Literacy Survey of 1993, the skills of more than 40 percent of all American adults are below level 3—the level associated with annual earnings above the poverty line. The box titled "A Nation Lacking Skills" displays a breakdown of the literacy skills among workers, high school graduates, and college graduates. Comparable data on the adult deaf population are lacking. However, on the basis of information from school-age deaf children, we can surmise that the statistics for deaf adults are more dismal than those projected for the population as a whole.

In the early part of the twentieth century, education's major focus was on reading, writing, and arithmetic (also known as "the three Rs"). In the industrial economy of that time, there were high-paying jobs in sectors such as manufacturing that did not require high literacy skills and thus provided many opportunities for the less qualified. Today, information and knowledge are growing at a far more rapid rate than ever before, and workers are now often required to be familiar with technical data and have more specialized skills. Consequently, the meaning of knowledge has shifted from being able to

---

Fast Facts on Literacy

- Forty-four million Americans age sixteen and older have the lowest literacy skills (level 1) and have significant literacy needs.
- Forty-three percent of people with the lowest literacy skills live in poverty.
- Seventy percent of people with the lowest literacy skills have no full- or part-time job.
- Workers lacking a high school diploma earn $452 per month compared to $1,829 for college graduates.
- Eight million people (4 percent of the total adult population) were unable to perform even the simplest literacy tasks.

Source: National Institute for Literacy

A Nation Lacking Skills

Literacy Skills	U.S. Workers	High School Graduates	College Graduates
Inadequate	41%	50%	15%
Adequate	34%	38%	39%
Excellent	25%	14%	46%

Note: About 40 percent of adult workers have inadequate literacy skills, 50 percent of high school graduates lack the skills required to do a job adequately, and even graduating from college offers no guarantee that a person has good literacy skills.

Source: National Institute for Literacy

store and recall information to being able to find it and use it (Simon 1996). If adults are to fit into the new economy, it is thought that they must be able to think and read critically, express themselves clearly, and be adept at problem solving. Economists tell us that today, in order to secure a well-paying job in a high-performance organization, adults will need all of these skills as well as ninth-grade-level or higher skills in reading, mathematics, and computing. These same economists predict that the jobs that will grow the fastest are the ones that will require more education and more training than ever before. They also cling strongly to the forecast that future economic growth will depend heavily on a workforce that is highly literate.

The Effects of Low Literacy Skills

The current low status of literacy in the United States is such that millions of dollars have been invested in programs that are aimed at helping individuals acquire the skills that will enable them to compete in what has become a global economy, to exercise their rights and responsibilities, and to participate in their children's education.

Educational support that begins in the home is important because it enables children to meet the challenges they face at school. Demographic data show that one of the strongest predictors of a child succeeding at school is the educational attainment of the primary caregiver. We must add, however, that parents with any level of education can foster a home environment that is conducive to the development of literacy skills and success in school. Later chapters of this book show how this can be done.

In addition to lower earnings and poorer chances for advancement on the job, adults with low levels of literacy often lack the skills required to explore and use health-related information on prevention and detection of disease. Epidemiological studies have consistently shown a strong relationship between literacy and health: The lower the level of literacy, the worse the health.

Literacy also seems to be related to civic responsibilities and community activities. More than half of those with low levels of literacy do not vote in federal, state, or local elections nor do they participate in faith-based or secular organizations that provide support services. People with lower levels of literacy are also overrepresented in prison; when released, they are often unable to find employment partly due to poor literacy skills, and many become repeat offenders. However, those who participated in literacy programs while in jail usually have a better chance of rehabilitation.

Much has been written in favor of literacy, and a great deal of attention and money have been dedicated to the improvement of national standards although no one has yet been able to confirm the expectation that higher literacy levels will lead to greater individual happiness and well-being. On the other hand, we have to conclude, at the very least, that low levels of reading, writing, and computing may well present a formidable barrier to full participation in modern-day living. An important aspect of the new era of information technology is that not only does it require a high level of the three Rs but also a range of thinking skills. These include the ability to organize, analyze, evaluate, and use information in the home, at work, and in the community. This logical and reflective thinking has been labeled "literate thought," and it can only be reached by acquiring the fundamental skills of reading and writing.

Information technology has no doubt increased the demand for workers with very high skills; it has created new jobs, and even raised the skill requirements in other tasks that are only remotely connected to information technology. Inevitably, this has led to an increasing demand for further education, but the flip side of this situation is that the technology itself can provide a convenient vehicle for innovative instruction in both literacy and literate thought. Computers may well prove to be an adaptable resource in promoting reading, writing, language comprehension, educational qualifications, professional skills, and cognitive abilities that will help an individual attain the survival skills necessary to cope with modern-day life.

Currently, literacy has become a popular topic with newspapers, magazines, and talk shows on radio and TV. In these media, literacy has generally become a synonym for a wide range of favorable values ranging from patriotic fortitude and religious virtue to job competency, security, happiness, intellectual ability, and good health. Illiteracy has been depicted as a great plague, an unjust handicap, a menace to society, and has become synonymous with a host of negative attributes that include delinquency, criminality, immorality, incompetence, insecurity, unhappiness, and sickness. It has been widely predicted that, in the near future, there will be no jobs for the illiterate, and that an upgrading of literacy skills will be essential for increased productivity.

In sum, literacy can be viewed as a continuum. At one end is *functional literacy*, which involves the acquisition of those skills necessary to decode information in newspapers, instructional manuals, and simpler texts. At a higher level, *cultural literacy* refers to the acquisition of historical knowledge and a body of literature that enables informed participation in the social and political life of a culture. And at the high end is *critical literacy*, defined as the ability to decode ideological dimensions of information, which permits the analysis and formulation of those prescriptions required to build a better society.

It is only when all aspects of this continuum receive consideration that parents and teachers can make accurate decisions about what should count as literacy, for whom it should be available, when it should be offered, and in what kind of setting. The task of seeking out the sociocultural aspects of literacy, as they apply to the population of Deaf people and to general society, may be more profitable than the search for the causes of illiteracy in an attempt to eradicate it.

Deaf Children and Literacy

We begin this section with an indictment of our efforts to teach deaf children to read and write. Since the founding of the first school for deaf children in the United States in 1817, many different communication approaches have been used in the classroom. These approaches typically inspired much controversy in the field, such as discussions about the use of signing only or speech only. When signing was used, educators have argued whether it should be ASL, some form of English signing, or some combination of both. Where oral communication has been favored, educators have debated whether speechreading should be emphasized during communication or whether emphasis should be placed on the optimal use of residual hearing. (We could add to the fray Cued Speech, which is the use of hand signals that cue speech sounds and help people speechread, but only a very small percentage of programs ever subscribed to this method.) Currently oral programs are pressuring parents into deciding between the use of hearing aids and cochlear implants as a means for facilitating the acquisition of spoken language.

What have we achieved as a result of all these discussions? We have learned that deaf children are leaving school with language skills that are grossly underdeveloped and, in many cases, are not even achieving functional literacy. The first educational survey by Pitner and Patterson (1916) found that fourteen- to fifteen-year-old deaf children had an average reading age of seven years. That picture has changed little over the past eighty-five years despite the adoption of various methods and techniques that proponents claimed would provide the necessary and sufficient support for deaf children's literary development.

Parents, however, should not become confused, despondent, or disheartened at such tidings but rather see these numbers as a challenge that they can help their deaf children overcome. It has often been said that literacy, like charity, begins at home, and we know that many of those deaf children who succeeded in school had parents who optimized the language environment for them. You can have a tremendous influence on how well your deaf child will learn, and, as will be discussed in the following chapters, there is much that you can do at home to ensure that your child will grow up to be literate in an increasingly literacy-oriented society. See the box titled "A Day in the Life of Steve" for an example of how a deaf adult uses the printed word throughout his or her daily life.

Literacy and Communication

What teachers should be doing (and what parents should desire) is teaching reading and writing in the context of helping deaf children become competent communicators. Proficient readers and writers use their knowledge and skills to nurture an ever-expanding ability to communicate more effectively. Their interpretation of written passages goes beyond the face value of each individual word. Good readers, for example, supplant the literal meaning of a sentence by deciphering an author's intended meaning. This is illustrated in our everyday reading experiences, including reading newspapers, shopping lists, TTY phone calls, books, and captioned TV.

Newspapers

A quick scan of the newspaper will reveal many instances where the ability to read the words on a page is insufficient to understanding the sentence. Take the following sentence from *The Globe and Mail:*

> Years of patiently stockpiling draft choices put the Avs in a position
> to pay a premium to acquire the required commodities. (Duhatschek
> 2001)

A Day in the Life of Steve

Before going to work at a college, Steve checks the calendar to see what his two hearing children will be doing that day. He sees that, in the evening, he and his wife will be driving their daughter to a basketball practice and a piano lesson and that he is coaching his son's baseball team. He scribbles a note to his wife to purchase a new baseball bat and make a dentist appointment for one of the children. At work, he spends the first twenty minutes reading and responding to e-mail messages and then begins reading journals to prepare for a lesson that he has to teach the next day. At 11:00, he makes a TTY call to a colleague to remind him that they have a racquetball game at noon. His colleague types back LUNCH S ON ME IF U REACH DOUBLE DIGITS C U AT NOON GA TO SK

At 1:00 p.m., Steve attends a meeting where a real-time reporter is present to type all that is being said by the hearing faculty members of his department. At 2:15 p.m., his daughter pages him to remind him to check a book out of the library. The message appears on the LCD display of his pager.

Steve buys the newspaper as he leaves his office building and stops at a bank to fill out an application form for a new credit card. At home, he relaxes for a half hour watching the local news, which is captioned. His children tell him to turn the sound on so that they can watch the news too. After an evening of driving the children around, he settles down to chat with the family and catch up on some reading. At 10:00 p.m., he receives a fax from his sister querying him about his upcoming visit to her place. Shortly after, his wife hands him a list of garden supplies that he needs to buy the next day. He highlights the day's events in his daily journal and then picks up a novel that he only reads just before going to sleep.

"What on earth does this mean?" could be the first question someone would ask after reading this sentence. But avid hockey fans would readily decipher the sentence's meaning as well as the author's intention. They would be able to do this without reading the rest of the article. For others, reading the rest of the article would be necessary to glean most of the background information needed to interpret the sentence (but being a well-read sports fan would certainly be a big advantage). In the sentence, "Avs" is an abbreviation for "Avalanche," as in the Colorado Avalanche of the National Hockey League. The phrase "stockpiling draft choices" is a reference to a practice where a team will trade players to other teams and receive future draft choices in return. In this way, they can accumulate future draft picks one, two, or more years in advance. Teams in need of young, high-caliber players covet draft choices in the first or second round; therefore, a team with a lot of draft choices on the books can pay a high price ("pay a premium") to get the type of players they want ("the required commodities") by trading their draft choices. And what about the sportswriter's reference to the Avs's practice of stockpiling draft choices? The implication is that the Avs will have a strong team for years to come because they have the assets available to acquire the players they need to do this.

When reading the above sentence, a good reader who is unfamiliar with trading practices in hockey or who lacks familiarity with sportswriters' terminology will realize that more information is needed and will also know how to extract this information from the context of the newspaper article.

Shopping Lists

What could be simpler than reading a list of things to buy? There is no grammar involved, and the intended reader will likely recognize the items listed. But even a list of words can call forth more than just knowing what the words are.

Good writers are able to communicate their thoughts clearly, and the intent of their message is unmistakable. They use the context of a situation and knowledge of their intended reader to influence how they pen their messages. They write to achieve certain objectives, but the same message may be written quite differently depending upon the intended audience. Thus, a wife might write the following simple grocery list for her spouse:

Asparagus

Cheese

Milk

Tea

Dill

Her husband interprets the list as,

1 bunch of asparagus

1/2 pound of sharp cheddar cheese

1 gallon of 2% organic milk

A box of green tea

A jar of dill weed

To a stranger, however, this shopping list will be ambiguous and result in questions about how much asparagus; what kind of cheese, milk, and tea; whether dill refers to the spice or the pickle; and if it's the spice then is it dill weeds or dill seeds? The wife does not need to indicate the particulars and measurement of each item listed for her husband because she knows he will correctly interpret what she has written down. Likewise, the husband is drawing from his bank of prior experiences to understand the intended meaning of the list.

TTY Phone Call

The TTY, or teletype, made its appearance in the Deaf community in the 1960s (Lang 2000). Invented by Robert Weitbrecht, a Deaf man, the TTY had the same effect on deaf people as the phone had on hearing people when it was introduced to homes and businesses across the country over one hundred years ago. Both instruments are used for communicating thoughts albeit in two different mediums.

The TTY relies on printed messages that appear on paper or on an LCD display. With the TTY, reading and writing once again come into play in a deaf person's life. Let's examine the message shown in the box titled "A Day in the Life of Steve."

LUNCH S ON ME IF U REACH DOUBLE DIGITS C U AT NOON
GA TO SK

We know from the context of the TTY call that the person who typed this message is talking about playing racquetball in which a game is played until one of the players reaches twenty-one points. The phrase DOUBLE DIGITS refers to numbers with two digits in them. To REACH DOUBLE DIGITS, a player would have to score at least ten points. The writer of this message is playfully mocking the other person's skills as a racquetball player and is in effect saying, "If you can score ten points against me, then I will gladly buy you lunch," with the unwritten implication "It ain't gonna happen."

TTY users seldom type in punctuation marks and therefore, the apostrophe is omitted in the contraction of "lunch is," which results in LUNCH S instead of LUNCH'S. The first U is obviously short-hand for *you*, and the letters C U are a short way to say *see you*. Finally, the phrase GA TO SK is a standard notation used when a person is ready to end a TTY message. The GA means *go ahead*, and the SK means *stop keying*. With this message the writer is essentially saying, "I have nothing more to say, and I am ready to hang up. You can say something or end this message."

Many deaf people will attest to the positive influence that using a TTY has had on their reading and writing skills. But as the above message indicates, the reading and writing component is but one part of the skills needed to communicate on a TTY.

On-line Chats

The Internet is rapidly replacing the telephone as a teenager's means of talking to friends. But on-line dialogue is not simply a matter of writing down what one wants to say in English. Just as with TTY conversations, a code for on-line typing has evolved, perhaps through the young people's desire to speed up a communicating process made slower through the necessity of typing as well as their practice of simultaneously carrying on a conversation with seven, eight, or more people. Below is an actual transcript of two children's conversation, including their use of spelling, punctuation, and capitalization. For the benefit of the uninitiated, we have inserted in brackets the meaning of the abbreviations.

Rebecca: What up
Jenny: nm u? [not much, you?]
Rebecca: nuttin, just chillen
Jenny: coo   [cool]
Rebecca: Did you hear what happened yesterday?
Jenny: No
Rebecca: The gym teacher got fired
Jenny: OMG [Oh my God! or Oh my goodness!]
Jenny: Why?
Rebecca: He put a dead rattlesnake on the principal's chair.
Jenny: OMG! For real?
Rebecca: naw jk   [No, just kidding]
Jenny: LOL   [laughing out loud]
Rebecca: brb [be right back]
Jenny: k   [ok]
Rebecca: Back
Jenny: Where'd ya go
Rebecca: My dad was coming, I had to look busy reading
Jenny: hahahaha
Rebecca: oh, here he comes again. . . .G2G   [Got to go]
Jenny: c-ya, ttyl, bye   [See ya. Talk to you later.]

And they talk like this for hour upon hour. At the time of this dialogue, Rebecca was fourteen years old and Jenny twelve. Get used to it, because this way of communicating is more the norm among children than the exception.

Captioned TV

Closed captioning made its entry into the mundane of a deaf person's life in the mid- to late 1970s. It was hailed by all as a key to helping deaf people access a wider world of information. We feel that its importance in the development of literacy skills in deaf children is so great that chapter 6 is devoted to this topic. Here, we wish only to introduce you to a few language samples from captioned programs, both TV and videos. From *Action Man*, a cartoon,

> The crew abandoned the ship claiming to be attacked by mechanical bugs. I can stop the bugs from jamming the frequency except this bug is thinking one step ahead.

From *Chicken Run*, a movie,

> Or this little number. All the rage in the fashionable chicken coops of Paris. In my R.A.F. days we were never allowed to waste time with unnecessary chitchat.

From *A View to a Kill*, a James Bond movie,

> May Day: Someone will take care of you.
>
> 007: You will see to that personally, will you?

From the September 2, 2001, broadcast of *ABC Sunday Evening News*,

> His most loyal constituents may be erased by redistricting.
>
> It will be a forced retirement because his district will not be there for him to run.

From *Malcolm in the Middle*, a TV sitcom,

> Reese: You're too short to ride it.
>
> Dewey: I'm in the 40th percentile and you're too stupid to ride.

These sentences might look simple to an experienced reader. But a deaf child or even a deaf teenager can be challenged by each sentence's vocabulary, syntax, humor, idiom, innuendo, or jargon.

Books

One of the reasons that a deaf child's reading level appears to hit a ceiling at the fourth grade is that reading at this level becomes more inferential. That is, to understand what an author is saying, the reader has to infer the meaning from the written word. The following sentence from the children's classic *Big Red* by Jim Kjelgaard (1945) illustrates the importance of being able to make inferences whilst reading:

> The night was lifting slowly, reluctantly. (139)

Even without context in which to place this sentence, experienced readers will surmise that someone has been waiting for a long time for day to break; that it is taking longer for the morning light to appear than this person had anticipated. But even with context—a boy is going deer hunting—the sentence might still appear to be vague. The passage before this sentence, however, helps clear up the meaning:

> Danny was up long before dawn the next morning. He milked and fed the cow, fed Asa, cooked breakfast for himself, gave Ross what he wanted, and packed a lunch. . . . Then he filled his rifle with five cartridges, dropped five more into his pocket, and with Red crowding close beside him went out on the porch. The night was lifting slowly, reluctantly. (139)

With this added information, we know that Danny is anxious for the sun to come up so he can begin hunting. *Big Red* has a fifth-grade reading level, but almost every page requires the reader to infer the meaning of at least one passage.

So this is what literacy is about: Knowing how to interpret, analyze, and synthesize the writings of other people while being able to express oneself in script in a manner that is appropriate for the context of the message and the intended audience. It requires a large vocabulary, fluency in the use of grammar, an understanding of the cultural information embedded in the language, an understanding of the social context surrounding a message, and the expert ability to integrate all of these features almost instantaneously.

Learning to use print as an effective form of communication is a challenge for everyone, deaf and hearing, and in the quest to teach literacy to deaf children, we are often guilty of overlooking the complex nature of the reading and writing process. Much emphasis is placed on the acquisition of the first language in a spoken or signed form. This is an important emphasis, because all deaf children should have access to language at an early age. Nevertheless, it is a fallacy to think that reading will automatically grow with language development. The acquisition of a language, English or ASL, does not guarantee that a person will be a proficient reader and writer or even be literate. Evidence for this is to be found in the thousands of hearing children who have mastered spoken English but cannot read. There are also Deaf children of Deaf parents who learned ASL as infants yet have difficulty expressing themselves in print or understanding what others have written. Further evidence can be found among top executives of Fortune 500 companies whose mastery of the spoken word is in sharp contrast to their inability to articulate clear thoughts on paper; or among those university graduates who are unable to write a decent description of a movie they have just watched. Yet, both of these latter groups of people have mastered the use of spoken English.

Challenges to Literacy Development

What then can parents do to help their deaf children become literate? Answering that question is the purpose of this book. But first it may be helpful to provide a brief initiation to the key challenges that literacy development presents to deaf children.

There Are a Lot of English Words to Learn

We tend to take for granted the size of our vocabulary while not realizing the extent of it. Stewart and Kluwin (2001) made the following observation:

> There are 10,000 words or so in our everyday speech. And the
> average adult can recognize between 70,000 and 120,000 words. If
> you are ever stuck for a word, then the *Oxford English Dictionary* has
> thousands of them of them standing by. In fact, it has over 450,000
> entries in a set of volumes that is about three feet wide standing side
> by side. A new edition is in the works, when many more entries will

be added. With steady injections of ingenuity and a few decades of leisure time, you can use affixes and other linguistic tools to expand this number to over 2,000,000 words. In sheer volume, no other language in the world comes anywhere close to having a vocabulary half the size of English. (78)

With so many words in the English language, it is obvious that schools cannot be the only source for helping deaf children expand their vocabulary. Parents have to pitch in to help their deaf children learn new words, and they can do this by providing experiences that will expose their children to these words and give them opportunities to use them. Although reading can and does help deaf children acquire new vocabulary, it is the use of words in their everyday communication that is most effective in helping them during the initial stages of their acquisition of language.

English Is a Spoken Language

Even with the use of hearing aids and cochlear implants, deaf children do not have enough hearing to allow them to converse freely in speech. Not having full access will hinder their acquisition of language. And learning to read and write while simultaneously learning English will slow down the process of becoming literate. The flip side of this equation is that some deaf children are able to use their literacy skills to help them acquire English. Still, the lack of access to a spoken language will, for the most part, make it difficult for deaf children to learn to read and write.

Children Are Active Participants in the Construction of Their Language

Just listening to speech or watching someone sign does not, by itself, lead to the acquisition of speech or signing skills. Children must actively participate in the communication process in order to access the meaning of what is being said and to learn that what they say can engender a response from others. Deaf children must understand the function of communication before they will be receptive to the use of reading and writing as a viable means of communicating with others. In other words, a deaf child will be more receptive and motivated to learn to read and write if his participation in this type of communication leads to desirable results.

Children Learn Language by Using It

Children, like adults, typically say things because they are looking for a result. The results might be external, such as getting a glass of milk when they ask for it or receiving a response to a question. Or it might be internal, as when two-year-olds scribble on a piece of paper. The act pleases them because they are doing something that they have seen their parents doing. Seldom, if ever, do children do something that has no purpose or intent. Muma and Teller (2001) point out that language will grow when children learn that the act of communication is a viable means for expressing their intent. Thus, the toddler will say "cookie" when he wants one. The teenage son writes a note to his parents pledging to do extra chores if he can have the keys to the car on Saturday night. Seldom will the toddler say "cookie" once he has received the cookie. Nor do we find many teenagers writing notes to their parents once they have the car keys in hand other than to say, "Gone to a movie. Back at midnight. Please don't stay up."

The Transition to Print Owes Its Origin to a Spoken Language or a Signed Language or Both

We are not going to enter into the arguments about which language or method of communication parents should use, although in later chapters, we do introduce some of the key considerations that parents must deal with when making the decision about how to communicate with their deaf children. Here, we wish only to emphasize that the communication used at home will have some effect on a child's acquisition of language and subsequent development of literacy skills.

The critical variable under discussion here is exposure to language. When parents communicate with their child in a language, it is important that deaf children understand what is being communicated. This means that they must have access to the code (e.g., signs, speech sounds, print) in which a language is expressed. Without access to the code, a language cannot be learned fluently.

The fact that ASL does not have a written component should not detract from its value in literacy development. ASL is a language that is readily accessible to deaf children at a young age. The language skills that deaf children learn using ASL can be transferred to their learning of English. Thus, whether parents selected English or ASL as their home language, the key is for the child to develop proficiency in this language at an early age so that he will be better prepared—linguistically—for handling the transition to communicating in print.

You should keep in mind that decisions about the choice of language will depend on the competencies demonstrated by the child who must be monitored at regular intervals. A periodic review of the choice of language and the conditions for learning should always remain a viable option no matter which approach to literacy is initially adopted at home or later at school.

Conclusion

Literacy means to understand and use written information in daily activities at home, in the community, and in the workplace to achieve one's goals and to develop one's knowledge and potential. Millions of dollars have been spent to improve national standards because low levels of literacy are likely to present barriers to full participation in modern American life. The overall level of literacy in the United States is a cause for concern, and the level for deaf children is also far too low.

If deaf children are to achieve higher levels of literacy, they will need to be taught reading and writing in the context of becoming competent communicators. The key challenges that literacy presents to them are (1) the acquisition of a large vocabulary, (2) the learning of reading and writing while simultaneously learning English, (3) active participation in the communicative process, (4) the learning of language through usage, and (5) the choice of language. The rest of the book aims to assist parents in taking an active role in helping their child meet these challenges.

CHAPTER 2

How Do Children Acquire Language?

This chapter will help you understand

- What language is
- The terms used to describe aspects of language
- Normal stages of language development
- Whether language is learned or taught
- The communication systems used by deaf children

Language is the all-important variable in the development of literacy skills in deaf children. Researchers will tell you that those deaf children who are successful readers and writers had a solid foundation in language before they were able to develop their literacy skills. Yet, many teachers extol the benefits of literacy programs in helping children to learn English. According to these educators, as children read, they pick up new vocabulary and learn about sentence patterns, the use of phrases, and other features of the English language. These contrasting points of view can confuse the parents of a deaf child who simply want to know what they can do to help their child read and write.

Many deaf professionals will tell you that as they became better readers, their journey to master the English language was given a significant boost. They will also tell you that they already had acquired a significant amount of language and a certain degree of fluency in English, American Sign Language (ASL), or both before they began to read. This connection between literacy and language development is illustrated in the following story about Kathleen.

Kathleen is a doctoral student at a major U.S. university. She obtained all of her schooling in an oral environment. Beginning at six or seven years old, her mother (a high school teacher) had her write down each day what she had done at school. The mother would read what was written, talk about it, make one or two corrections to the writing, and then have Kathleen read the corrections. This ritual took place regularly throughout her elementary school years. Kathleen points to this experience of writing, talking, and correcting as key factors in her acquisition of English. However, she is quick to add that she must already have acquired a lot of language, because she was able to discuss what she had written to her mother.

Kathleen's experience as a deaf child learning English is not unique. For many, if not all, deaf individuals, language learning and literacy development are interdependent and not exclusive of one another.

What Is Language?

Whenever there are discussions about literacy, the word *language* will crop up and have different meanings for different people. In this book, *language* simply means any symbol system used by humans to communicate with each other. The word is derived from the Latin *lingua*, meaning "tongue," so it is perhaps not surprising that language and speech are often confused. These two terms, however, are not interchangeable. Speech is but one of the codes through which a language such as English or Ukrainian is transmitted, whereas print is a graphic code for many of our spoken languages. In addition to speech and print, signing is another means of expressing a language. ASL and Zimbabwe Sign Language are just two examples of the many languages articulated by the hands and expressed in a visual-spatial medium.

Every culture has a language, and the estimated total number of languages in the world is somewhere between 3,000 and 6,000 depending on who is counting and how they do it. Even though the languages are all different, they do have several things in common. Each language consists of a symbol system that is used for communication among people in the same culture, and that system permits the production of an infinite number of utterances using a finite number of words and rules. For many centuries, the study of language has received a great deal of attention but, even so, today we are left with many unanswered questions and many questionable answers. Indeed, it would be true to say that we still don't fully understand how children acquire language.

Throughout this book, we shall be concerned with English and, to a lesser extent, ASL. Our greater concern with English stems from the fact that this book is about how parents can help their deaf children acquire literacy, which, in its simplest form, is the ability to read and write. However, we must note that English and ASL are quite different from one another. ASL is conveyed in a visual-spatial mode and has no spoken or generally accepted written form despite several attempts to create one.[1]

The process of writing down English word equivalents (called *glosses*) for each ASL sign has been used to study the grammar of ASL; however, this method undervalues both the manual and non-manual aspects of a sign language because written glosses can be misleading, ambiguous, or even inaccurate.[2] The difficulty of using glosses is shown in the following sentence with the glosses noted on the second line:

English: Do you want more potatoes?

ASL: MORE POTATOES WANT YOU?

In the English sentence, it is the grammar and selection of words that tells us a question has been asked. In the gloss of how this question might be asked following ASL grammatical structure, it is the question mark at the end of the sentence that tells us it is a question. What the gloss does not show is that when asking a yes/no question in ASL, the signer tilts his head forward while raising the eyebrows; these facial cues (also referred to as facial grammar) signal that a question is being asked.

Even though most things that can be said in English can be translated into sign language, many of the ASL signs cannot be matched with a single English word. The visual-spatial nature of sign language makes it a unique and systematic language and one that is distinct from the auditory-vocal pattern of English.

English, on the other hand, can be spoken, printed, signed, finger-spelled, or expressed in Morse code or Braille. But even though English and ASL are different, they are not incompatible, and although it may be difficult for a deaf child to learn more than one language, it is possible.

Aspects of Language

According to the vast literature on language acquisition and discussions with teachers, clinicians, and other parents, during such occasions as planning an Individual Family Service Plan or an Individual Educational Plan, several aspects of language will receive attention. They include

Phonology—the sounds of a language

Morphology—the structure of words

Lexicon—the vocabulary

Syntax—the structure of phrases and sentences

Semantics—the study of meaning, and finally

Pragmatics—the way language is used in a social context

This list has an ominous ring to it that suggests a tedious and involved discussion on modern grammar will follow. That will not be necessary. The brief descriptions below will show that most readers are already familiar with these aspects of language, though they may not be aware of the names that linguists have attached to them.

Phonology

Phonology is the study of the sounds, or phonemes, of a language. English has forty-two basic sounds that do not have much meaning when articulated in isolation. For example, the phonemes /c/, /a/, and /t/ by themselves mean very little, but all three in combination produce the word *cat*, which does have a meaning. The assignment of that particular meaning to those three sounds is quite arbitrary. If we alter one of these sounds, we can change the original word to *mat, cut, cap, hat, pat, fat,* or *cot.* An amazing fact emerges from the study of phonemes: In English, with a few more than two score sounds, we can produce hundreds of thousands of words already in use, and others that are yet to be created.

Morphology

Morphology is the study of words, or more precisely, the study of morphemes, which are the smallest meaningful units of language. Every word in English consists of one or more morphemes. The word *cat* consists of one morpheme; but the word *cats* consists of two: *cat* and *s.* Moreover, both morphemes are distinguishable in that *s* is a bound morpheme, because although it carries the meaning of more than one (plural), it cannot stand alone like the other morpheme *cat.*

Within this field of study also fall the rules for applying morphemes called suffixes at the ends of words (e.g., *-ment, -ed, -ly*), the rules for applying morphemes called prefixes at the beginnings of words (e.g., *un-, dis-, re-*), and the rules for building compound words (e.g., *house-boat, cow-boy*).

Lexicon

The lexicon is a language's vocabulary or dictionary and consists of the words we use to make phrases and sentences. English is divided into (a) content words that have meaning and represent objects, persons, events, and actions and (b) function words such as *a, the, to, for,* and *with,* which, by themselves, have little or no meaning yet give precision to phrases and sentences. As indicated earlier, English has the largest lexicon of all the world's languages.

Knowing words, however, is not the only thing we need in acquiring a language nor is it the most important. We can know the meaning of every content word in the English language and still be unable to communicate adequately with other users of English until we discover the way to produce phrases and sentences, or in other words, until we acquire syntax.

Syntax

The syntax of a language is the way words are put together to make grammatical sentences. As children, we learned at an early age how to produce sentences, but for the most part, we were not conscious that we were learning syntactical rules. In other words, we learned linguistic rules that we could apply and work with but could not identify or articulate. We knew that "Home little the went boy" was not a grammatical sentence, whereas "The little boy went home" was acceptable. And we could readily make this decision without ever having heard of a noun phrase (*the little boy*), a verb phrase (*went home*), an irregular verb (*went*), or an adverbial (*home*).

Syntax, or the arrangement of word order, becomes important in English because, unlike some other languages, English has few inflections to mark the important words or signify their grammatical roles. Hence, modern grammar examines the way we make changes to basic sentences by adding, subtracting, deleting, rearranging, or joining words to produce an infinite number of simple and complex sentences (Roberts 1967). It is a fascinating area of grammar; for those who wish to venture further, Virginia Heidinger's (1984) self-instructional approach to syntax would make a good starting point.

A general characteristic of a language is that words are not directly combined into sentences but into intermediate units called *phrases,* which are then combined into a sentence. In this way, phrases establish important internal relationships. How this occurs is shown in the following sentence:

The naughty girl/pushed/the little boy/with red hair.

The phrases behave like units and stay intact even when the sentence is rearranged, as in the passive transformation.

The little boy/with red hair/was pushed by/the naughty girl.

Semantics

Semantics refers to the meanings and relationships that are expressed in a sentence. For example, the sentences "The mother surprised her daughter" and "The daughter surprised her mother" both have the same morphemes and the same syntax but very different meanings. In simplest terms, semantics tells us what sentences mean. It does this by specifying the relationship between the words and the phrases in sentences. For our purposes, semantics is meaning, and meaning is obtained through the way we use words and phrases in a sentence.

Pragmatics

Pragmatic concepts refer to the use of language, the reasons for communicating, and the purposes underlying the production of an utterance. They include the various functions of language, and these are many. Requests, commands, comments, questions, answers, protests, repetitions, arguments, greetings, discussions, and the like are but a few of the many ways we interact when communicating in social situations.

Discourse: The Ultimate Goal of Language

The phonological, morphological, syntactical, semantic, and pragmatic components of language briefly discussed above may be looked at separately as we have done, but in communication and real life, these aspects are not isolated but are inextricably bound together. Just as sounds are brought together according to certain rules to form words, and words are combined to form sentences, then sentences must be linked together to form a narrative. This is called discourse.

Linguists study discourse in written language (texts) and also in conversation. When we request information, tell a story, offer an explanation, describe an object or event, or share our thoughts with another person, we generally use several sentences, and these are held together by certain conventions; otherwise our communication would break down. The rules for discourse are quite complex but are readily learned. In our society, for example, most people know how to start a conversation, when to speak, when to listen, how and where to look, how to change the subject, what kind of body language and facial expression to use, and when to end a conversation. Discourse is important because through it, all children, deaf and hearing, acquire language and knowledge—two basic ingredients for the successful development of literacy skills (Stubbs 1983).

From Discourse to Language Acquisition

The importance of discourse is further stressed by those linguists who believe that we are born with a language acquisition device and that we are wired or programmed to learn a language if we have access to it at an early age. According to them, we don't have to learn any rules. All we need to do is to hear or see people using a language and we will learn it. The key to building a vocabulary is to make the connection between the word (or sign) and the object or concept to which it refers. Hence, if a deaf child never hears a word, sees a word, or sees a sign, then the word or sign will not become part of his lexicon. Syntax, on the other hand, is different. A child does not have to hear or see a sentence before he can make it. We are all constantly creating new sentences that may never have been spoken or written before. This is because we are born with something that helps us acquire language (provided we are exposed to the rules and can access them). Similarly, we must be exposed to the other aspects of language in a variety of situations to become proficient language users.

For language to be learned effectively, certain conditions must be met. At the very least a child must have the following:

- Access to the language. This implies that the child must be able to receive and process the language's codes or symbols (signs, speech, or print). If a child is unable to receive sufficient auditory signals to process speech then his chances of acquiring fluency in spoken English are minimal. Similarly, if a child cannot visually process signed information then he will likely not acquire proficiency in ASL. See the box titled "When Language Is Learned Too Late," for

---

When Language Is Learned Too Late

It is generally accepted that if a child has not acquired proficiency in a signed or spoken language by the age of ten to twelve years then they will likely never acquire fluency in any language to which they might be exposed. An extreme example of this is shown in the story of Chelsea, who was born deaf in a remote area of northern California, but her deafness was misdiagnosed as a developmental disability.

Chelsea grew up shy, dependent upon others, and without language, but she was cared for by a loving family. When she was thirty-one years old, her deafness was finally discovered, and Chelsea was fitted with hearing aids that helped her hear speech sounds. Intensive habilitation brought her to the point where she knew approximately 2,000 words, but her syntax remained bizarre, and she was unable to correctly produce even one complex sentence.

The case of Chelsea and others like her clearly demonstrates that there is a critical period for the acquisition of syntax (Curtiss 1989).

---

a story about a girl who did not receive access to language symbols until later in life.

- Exposure to the language as early as possible. This is true for all children. It has been said that if a child has not acquired a language by the time he reaches ten to twelve years of age, he might never acquire fluency in any language. See the box titled "Timing Makes All the Difference!" for the story of one girl who acquired grammatically correct language although she was not exposed to it until the age of six years and the story of another girl who did not acquire a proficient command of language because she did not begin hearing it until she was twelve years old.

- Proficient language role models in speech and/or signs. These models are the parents and other adults and peers who communicate with children in a variety of situations, thereby demonstrating

Timing Makes All the Difference!

It does matter when a child is exposed to language. Children in Belgium and northern parts of France often learn up to five languages by the time they are five years old merely from exposure to these languages in their everyday lives. The language is not taught to them; rather, they absorb language from the adult speakers around them. But what happens when there is no early exposure to language? Well, it seems that the answer to this question depends, as illustrated in the stories about Genie and Isabelle below, on how early or how late the exposure comes.

Genie was a twelve-year-old abused child who was discovered in 1970 in a Los Angeles suburb. Up to this point, she had received almost no auditory or visual language symbols having been locked up in a room for her entire life. Once she was discovered, Genie received intensive therapy that has been recorded in a book by Rymer (1993), but because language learning did not take place within the critical window for developing language, Genie only learned to produce immature pidgin-like sentences.

Isabelle was six years old when she and her speechless brain-damaged mother escaped imprisonment in her grandparents' home. Eighteen months later, Isabelle had acquired approximately 1,500 words and was able to produce many grammatically correct complex sentences. The fact that she was exposed to language before the critical age of ten to twelve years seemed to have made a world of difference (Tartter 1986).

the pragmatic use of words and sentences. These proficient users of a language stimulate the growth of language in young children.
- Interactions with other children to develop the ability to see things from a different point of view. It is through play and association with other children that a child will learn to share, settle conflicts, cooperate, compromise, collaborate, and conform. In the case of learning sign language, exposure to peers who are fluent in ASL can also help overcome the lack of exposure to ASL in the home that many deaf children of hearing parents experience.

This final condition is especially critical because it highlights one of the fundamental dilemmas that deaf children of hearing parents face. Many of these deaf children cannot adequately receive and understand their parents' speech. Further, hearing parents are not normally proficient signers, and so their deaf child will receive inadequate representation of a signed language at home. In these particular cases, exposure to sign at school can help. This is seen in the story of Peter, whose deaf parents were not fluent ASL signers. His circumstances are similar to some extent, to the situation of deaf children who have hearing parents who sign (see box titled "Good Language Models Help").

When any or all of the above conditions are not present, children face an overwhelmingly more difficult time in trying to learn a language. And if learning a language is difficult, the task of learning to read and write is formidable.

Good Language Models Help

Peter is a nine-year-old profoundly deaf boy with deaf parents. But his parents did not learn to sign until they were in their late teens, and they acquired it poorly. Although Peter saw only his parents' defective ASL, it is reported (Singleton and Newport 1993) that his own signing was far superior and much closer to ASL. This performance was regarded as astounding and has been held up as an example of creolization by a single child. Moreover, there may be many more such cases. Ninety percent or more of deaf children are born to hearing parents, and many of these children, when young, may be exposed to sign that has been incompletely learned by their parents. Yet, it may be that these children, like Peter, will learn to convert the impoverished sign that they have learned in their homes into a richer language that approximates ASL. Interactions with their peers, teachers, and others who are fluent in ASL will help them to do so.

Stages of Language Development

Our approach to language development so far has focused on particular components, and although this permits an exploration of common linguistic terms, it doesn't make a great deal of sense for parents who observe their deaf child's language growth over time and not over areas of development. The remainder of this chapter will therefore shift to the chronology of language development in the early years leading up to literacy. A word of warning may be necessary because this approach could generate some unwarranted anxiety. There are children who do not achieve the milestones at the ages given here or who do not follow the same order of development as listed; yet many, if not all, of these youngsters will ultimately acquire fluency in language. Therefore, it must be kept in mind that this chronological approach only gives the approximate sequence that children follow in language acquisition and will cloud the fact that children vary enormously in their development. Parents should not view these stages as any kind of schedule but rather use these data to appreciate the marvels of children's language acquisition.

In our discussion of developmental stages, we are first going to describe how hearing children learn a spoken language and then follow this with a discussion of deaf children's language acquisition. At this point, however, it should be noted that the stages of development for deaf children who are exposed to ASL from birth parallel those of hearing children exposed to a spoken language.

In five short years after birth, children make incredible progress in language use. In their early years, they start with nonverbal communication (facial expression, body language, eye contact, sounds, and gestures) and then move rapidly to spoken (or signed) language, which is the most complex skill that we, as human beings, have developed. Even though babies do not say their first word until their first birthday or shortly thereafter, they start learning about language almost from birth. The foundations of communication and turn-taking develop in the first year of life, but even after a child begins to talk, much still needs to be learned about language and its uses. It takes several more years to fine-tune his comprehension of the spoken (and later written) word and to develop his vocabulary, grammar, conversational skills, and the ability to use language as a tool in learning and expressing ideas.

All children, it seems, are born with a built-in capacity to learn language. But although biologically programmed to develop language, they would not do so if they grew up isolated from communication with other people. The beginnings of successful communication arise from the relationship that exists between mother and child right from birth. The first interactions are mainly nonverbal—touching, caressing, and cuddling—that communicate care and love. The child gains a sense of security from the mother's touch, warmth, body language, and facial expression. Early and frequent contact provides a good environment for communication, and the more interaction between parent and child, the better that environment will be.

Communication, then, takes place long before the first word, and probably begins when a child returns a mother's smile or cries loudly when he wants something done about his current predicament. Although he will progress from heart-rending cries to a well-formed request, such as "I wanna go home 'cos I'm tired," in just a few years, there are some noticeable milestones along the way, and these are presented below.

Stage 1. Reflexive Communication: Birth to Three Months

This is a time of nonintentional communication to which the caregiver usually responds as if it really were intended. The infant does not, at this early stage, perform meaningful language acts because he is cognitively too immature to have any intent in mind. Indeed, the infant most likely has little idea that his behavior affects others. The mother or caregiver, however, automatically responds to the baby's sounds (crying, burps, sneezes, coughs, etc.), gestures, body movements, and facial expressions (smiles, frowns, eye movements, and gazes). Although these responses make it appear as if the baby is in fact communicating, the reality is that these acts are only reflex actions to urgent needs that the baby has (such as hunger or gas) or to stimuli in the environment. By about six weeks, however, the baby will "goo" when comfortably settled. Soon after, the mother can get the baby to goo increasingly by talking lovingly to him. Face to face with the child, the mother smiles and goos, and the baby smiles and goos right back. In this way, the feature of conversational turn-taking may begin very early in life.

Stage 2. Babbling: Three to Six Months

The baby still does not know that he can send a message in order to make something happen, but he puts together strings of vowels seemingly for his own pleasure. The vowel-like sounds that resulted quite early from swallowing and sucking movements now begin to decrease as syllables consisting of consonant-like sounds plus a vowel start to appear. His verbalizations, gestures, body language, and facial expressions become easier to interpret. He makes sounds and gives other clues that seem to communicate pleasure and displeasure. As yet, he still does not understand words, but he may comprehend gestures, such as extending his arms when he wants to be lifted, or situational contexts, such as knowing that being dressed up and placed in a baby buggy means an outing is imminent.

Stage 3. Intentional Communication: Eight to Twelve Months

Now the child begins to point, gesture, or produce meaningful sounds to gain attention or request something he wants. He may point and look at an object, make a sound or a gesture, and, if he does not get what he wants, he may even throw a tantrum. He begins to use sounds as if they were words ("Bob" may mean a toy or a bottle). He also begins to use a kind of jargon. At this stage, the caregiver often remarks that the child sounds like he is from a foreign country or a different planet.

Stage 4. First Words: Twelve to Eighteen Months

The child now uses a few words. Some of these refer to people (*dada* and *mom*), objects, events, and movements. Single words can have more than one meaning. *Mom* can mean "Pick me up mommy" or "This is mommy's bag." The child also uses words that are too narrow or too broad. *Bob* refers only to his bottle and no other bottle (underextension), whereas *dada* might refer not only to daddy but all males (overextension). Words are usually produced in isolation, and this stage can last from two months to a year. Many diaries have been kept of children's first words, and what is interesting is that the lists are similar. About half the first words said by children referred to food, clothing, household items, people, animals, and body parts, and the others were action words (*up, off, open*), modifiers (*all gone, more*), routines (*yes, no, bye-bye*), and chunks (*look that, have that*). His vocabulary increases slowly during this period because the child is putting a lot of time and effort into learning other important skills, such as standing and walking.

Stage 5. Two-Word Sentences: Eighteen to Twenty-Four Months

Sometime near his second birthday, when he may have a vocabulary of about forty words, the child begins to form two-word sentences such as "daddy car," which also has a variety of meanings, such as "I see daddy's car!" "There goes daddy's car!" and "I want to go in daddy's car!" Sometimes the child will mix the order of words, but conventional word order is soon learned. Now there is a large increase in vocabulary, which can grow to over one hundred words during this period. Parents report that the child seems to soak up language, and they find it hard to believe that he could have learned to use so many new words and come to understand so many others even out of context. Around this time, the child learns to negate. "No" will appear at the beginning of their two-word utterances as in "No daddy car!" Most parents can attest that "no" will be used more and more as he strives for independence and the right to do things for himself—even when he is not yet ready. This is also the time when parents will attempt brief conversations with him even though the child will generally not cooperate because, as yet, he has not learned how to carry on a conversation.

Stage 6. Three- to Four-Word Sentences: Twenty-Four to Thirty-Six Months

When about half the child's utterances are two-word sentences, he begins to form three-word sentences by (a) combining them—

"Daddy wash" and "Daddy car" become "Daddy wash car"—and by (b) addition and expansion—"A doggie" becomes "That a doggie" and "See car" becomes "See daddy car." Sentence length will increase as the child, through conversations, learns to use various parts of the English language, a process that includes using words incorrectly. These parts of the English language include

- Conjunctions (*and*)
- Prepositions (*in, on*)
- Auxiliaries (*can, will*)
- Plurals (*cars, foots*)
- Verb endings (*jumped, goed*)
- Copula (me *is*)
- Pronouns (*he, she, it*)
- Verbs (*wanna*)
- Quasi-modals (*gonna*)

And, as most parents will confirm, the "Why?" question is heard over and over again, probably to initiate a conversation, because it will take more time before he understands what "Why?" really means. This is also the time when a child shows that he loves stories and really enjoys being read to, particularly from well-chosen children's books.

Stage 7. Complex Sentences: Three to Five Years

The child has now arrived in a very short time to the point where he can combine two or more ideas. He first uses *and* to join phrases and sentences but soon adds *because, but, when, who, what,* and so forth to produce such sentences as "I can't eat it because I'm full." The child's grammar now becomes much more complex. The auxiliaries *can, will,* and *do* and correct forms of the copula (*is, are*) are used in questions. Contractions are used (*didn't, can't, I'm*). His spoken vocabulary can go as high as 5,000 words, and he appears to understand all that is said to him. He will still make the odd developmental error, such as overgeneralizing plurals (*sheeps*) and past tense (*catched*), but he will now begin to use language as a tool in problem solving, imagining, and learning. His conversations get longer, and narratives become part of his repertoire.

At about age three, children sometimes will attempt to tell a story—perhaps one or two sentences about a recent event, but with insufficient information for the listener to fully understand the situation. However, later in this stage, a big change occurs. The stories get longer (four or five sentences) and become well structured. Often the narrative has an introduction ("You know what happened to my dad?"), a background ("He was going to work"), a series of events ("He drove his car. He bashed into a bus. They towed the car away."), and an ending ("The garage men will fix it").

Stage 8. Literacy: Six+ Years

During this last stage, language growth and vocabulary in particular will continue to expand and develop as children discover the power of communication in all social interactions. However, the most articulate six-year-old is not even halfway there. He still has to develop further subtle phonological distinctions, more complex aspects of syntax and semantics, and finer discernments in both pragmatics and discourse (see also Grant 1987 and Owens 1988).

Now, or even earlier, attention can be given at home and school to the beginnings of reading and writing, which children need to acquire to become text literate. The building of these language skills requires, at minimum, the following:

1. A broad vocabulary
2. A good knowledge of syntax and other features of English
3. A store of background knowledge about the world in which we live

Equally important are the positive attitudes that can be passed on by parents who frequently read and write, are excited about books, and clearly show that they enjoy these activities. These parents will have children who, given the necessary and sufficient conditions, will want to read and write like their parents do because fervor and enthusiasm are highly contagious.

Language Is Learned

Because the complex process of language acquisition is so effortless for those children who can hear sufficiently to acquire a spoken language or for deaf children who are exposed to sign language, many people believe that children are predisposed to learn whatever language is spoken or signed around them. In other words, it would appear that for children who are exposed to accessible language from birth, language is learned rather than taught (Pinker 1984). The once-popular belief that parents taught their children language now belongs to folklore, and no one today would ask parents to give explicit lessons in language to their children. Indeed, it is highly unlikely that there are many parents who know enough grammar to do so.

It is also highly improbable that parental teaching could be responsible for their child's progress because his utterances on many occasions, while meaningful, are grammatically very different from those used by the parents. It's true that he gets a good head start from a universal variety of talk (motherese), commonly associated with the way mothers speak to their infants. This way of talking is characterized by a simplified vocabulary, repetitive utterances, and much give and take, but most of the credit goes to children's innate ability to learn language just from being exposed to it. This, however, is not meant to belittle in any way the importance of an authentic language environment.

The requirements for all children to acquire language are simple. A speaker or signer of the language must present sustained language experiences in a variety of situations that have real-life meaning. A soundtrack or video is not enough. At one time, deaf parents were strongly advised to expose their hearing children to TV for hours on end so the children would learn to speak and acquire English. This practice continued until it was discovered that in no cases did it help (Pinker 1994). Nor will it help if children rely solely on regularly scheduled language-learning lessons.

Finally, language experiences must be provided from an early age. Acquisition is guaranteed only to children less than six years old and is steadily compromised from this age to puberty, beyond which the chances of acquisition become much slimmer. The longer a child has to wait to learn, the harder it becomes.

Language and the Deaf Child

It is generally accepted that deaf children's language development follows a similar pattern to that of hearing children with the following caveat: They must be able to access the language they are learning. This means being able to see a language, as when a child is learning ASL, or, with the assistance of hearing aids and assistive listening devices, being able to hear most or all of a spoken language. There is also one exception to the pattern of development: Deaf babies (and hearing babies) who are exposed to sign language from birth begin to use their hands to make signs at approximately six months of age—well before children normally begin to articulate their first intelligible spoken words. See the box titled "From the Arms of Babies" for a discussion of how gesture likely preceded speech in the evolution of human language.

Obviously, whether parents want their deaf child to use signs or speech is an important decision and one that has implications for how and to what extent a child learns language. Despite the importance of this decision, this book is not geared to any particular communication method with deaf children. Throughout these

From the Arms of Babies

Babies who are signed to from birth are able to move their hands and form recognizable signs at six months of age or earlier, which is about four to six months before they say their first intelligible word. This occurs because babies are able to use their arms and hands to form meaningful gestures before they gain control of the organs associated with speech and is one of the reasons why linguists, such as the late William Stokoe, believed that signing "is a deeper older process than speech" (Stokoe 1978, p. 75).

pages, references will be made to the various methodologies, but the pros and cons will not be examined here for two reasons. First, even though it can be shown that each method of communication has had some degree of success with specific children, nowhere is there definitive evidence that one method will consistently give the best results for all deaf children. Second, there are many factors that clearly show that children with a hearing loss are not a homogeneous group. Diversity within the population of deaf children demands that we look at each individual deaf child rather than attempt to prescribe a single formula for the total population.

Having said that, we must, however, agree that there are some factors that are critical to the language development of all deaf children, and these include the following:

- Degree of hearing loss. Some hard of hearing children (or those who have a mild or moderate hearing loss) may receive sufficient gain from hearing aids that they are able to acquire a spoken language. But there is no guarantee that all hard of hearing children, even with hearing aids, will be able to adequately process sufficient speech sounds to become fluent users of a spoken language in a timely manner. Other children with severe or profound hearing loss may be better served learning sign language from an early age. Unfortunately, there is no way we can predict with any degree of accuracy which severe or profoundly deaf children will learn a spoken language through the use of amplified sound. All that we will say here about degree of loss is that, with the help of hearing aids, some deaf children will benefit a great deal from amplified sound, some will hear very little or nothing at all, and the remainder will fall somewhere in between.
- Age at onset of deafness. Prelingually deaf children are either born deaf or lose their hearing before they acquire language. Postlingually deaf children become deafened after they have begun to talk or even to read and write. Typically, the latter will have an easier task in learning a spoken language.
- Etiology. Some causes of deafness may lead to neurological damage or the presence of other disabilities.

- Time at diagnosis of hearing loss. Babies whose hearing loss is identified at an early age generally go on to learn language better than those who are diagnosed later. The earlier a hearing loss is diagnosed, the sooner decisions relating to communication can be made and support given to the parents. An early start also enables parents to create a home environment conducive to language learning.
- Ability of parent and child to communicate with each other. Whatever method of communication is used by the parents and child, it must be effective.
- Hearing status of parents. Hearing parents usually lean toward using speech as their primary means of communicating with a deaf child, whereas deaf parents are typically far more comfortable with signing.
- Parental acceptance of child's deafness. Parents who accept their child's deafness more readily proceed with the task of raising the child than parents who are in denial about their child's hearing loss or who refuse to make accommodations for their child in matters such as method of communication or need for visual information.

Given these foregoing factors and more, parents are faced with the challenge of how best to accommodate their deaf child's different abilities, attitudes, strengths, and weaknesses in order to give him the best possible opportunity for learning language. Therefore, it is helpful to look at some basic strategies that can be applied to all deaf children.

Language Grows from Language

There are things parents can do to increase the amount of language that their deaf child is exposed to and improve their overall manner of communication. Both of these events will help to encourage language growth.

Infants and Young Children

Patricia Spencer and her associates at Gallaudet University have studied the communication behavior of over one hundred families of both deaf and hearing infants ages three to twenty-eight months. They noticed that deaf parents' communicative behavior focused on providing their babies with visual information, a habit that did not come naturally to hearing parents (but could be taught). From this research, came the following four guiding principles for parents:

1. Engage in frequent, positive communication with your baby to help language develop faster. Take time to respond to your baby's needs, to let your baby know by your smiles and your touch that he is loved. Play and loving contact are almost as important as food to babies. Use as many senses as you can to send messages. Emphasize touching games. Move your body, face, and hands around in front of the baby. Emphasize your facial expressions even more than usual.

2. Be responsive—Follow the baby's lead. Notice where the baby is looking or in what the baby seems to be interested. Talk or sign about that object or activity.

3. Help babies see the communication and language that you are using. Especially with a young baby, often move your hand or body so he can see your communication while still looking at a toy or activity. Move an object (such as a toy) in front of the baby and then move it up toward your own face. When the baby can see your face and the object, talk about it. Tap on an object, perhaps several times, before and after you relate something about it. This helps the baby know what your communication is about. Tap the baby to signal "Look at me." Repeat the tapping signal or combine it with moving an object if your first try isn't successful. Remember that babies have to learn to look up when they are tapped.

4. Gradually modify your communication to make your baby's transition to language easier. When a baby shows that he or she is beginning to understand language, parents can start using very short sentences: one, two, or three words or signs at a time, plus pointing or tapping on objects. Repeat words, signs, or short sentences several times. Also tap on objects or point to activities to show the child what you are communicating about. (Spencer 2001, Laurent Clerc National Deaf Education Center Web site: http://clerccenter2.gallaudet.edu/kidsWorldDeafNet/e-docs/visual-conversations)

For all communication with infants and young children, Spencer emphasized that parents should be demonstrative in their use of facial expressions and body movements. At the earliest age, deaf infants have to sense their parents' excitement while talking to them. They have to learn to anticipate that someone is about to say something and to focus on that person's face. Facial expressions and body movements are every bit as important to a parent getting a message across as the actual words and signs themselves. Deaf parents who sign have little trouble using their faces to enhance their signing because facial expressions are a vital linguistic feature of ASL. Oral deaf adults also tend to have expressive faces when talking, because they too understand that visual cues are critical to language comprehension.

Older Children

Once deaf children have begun to use a language, it becomes imperative that parents create a home environment that is conducive to numerous conversations. The following are guiding principles for such an environment.

- Have a comfortable relationship with your child. Maintain a loving relationship so that your child feels secure being with you. Once you have established a good relationship, you will find that you really enjoy conversations with him, and both of you will seek out opportunities to "talk" to one another.
- Respond positively to your child's attempts to communicate. Language growth springs from practice. Be interested in what your child has to say to you and stimulate your conversations with questions that require more than just a "yes" or "no" response. Rather than "Ben, are you ready to leave now?" ask, "Ben, what else do you have to do before we leave?" Instead of "Is this a good program you're watching?" try "What is this program about?" or "Tell me what you like best about this program." This practice will encourage your child to be an active participant in discourse.
- Model correct language use rather than spending time correcting ungrammatical sentences. Children learn language in steps that increasingly approximate the grammar of mature language users. Accept the fact that what they say to you might not be perfect and focus on modeling good language in what you say to your child.

For example, if a child says, "I have to go swim now," refrain from correcting the sentence by saying, "You should have said, 'I have to go swimming now.'" Instead, respond with a model from which the child can learn: "Oh, you have to go swimming now." Do this whether your child uses English or ASL.

- Encourage self-expression. Not only do you want your child to feel comfortable talking to you, you also want him to use language as a way of expressing his feelings and thoughts, thinking aloud, formulating ideas, and offering explanations. Encourage him to feed his inquisitive mind by seeking answers to questions; get him to tell stories and jokes and much more. It is through this self-expression that he will learn the full value of language.

When parents make a consistent effort to communicate effectively with their deaf child, they are giving him the best opportunity for learning language, regardless of how they're communicating. However, not all methods of communication are appropriate for all deaf children. Therefore, if a deaf child is not making significant progress in acquiring language despite his parents' best efforts, they should review their method of communication with their child. This step may not be easy but it is critical.

Conclusion

Deaf and hearing children go through similar stages of language development, although the age at which they progress through these stages may vary. Deaf children's language acquisition is highly variable and dependent upon several factors that can influence their access to language and the rate at which it is acquired. Parents must select a method of communication to use with their deaf children and then take steps to ensure that their child is exposed to large amounts of language in a variety of settings, so that he may begin to learn new vocabulary and attain increasingly complex grammatical structures. At all times, parents should encourage their deaf child's attempts to communicate in signs or with words, and they should provide as many opportunities as they can for him to develop confidence in his ability to use language as a means of expressing himself. Parents must also be prepared to review the particular method of communication they have chosen (ASL, Signed English, speech, etc.) and be prepared to change their approach should circumstances dictate and before too much time has been wasted. Just remember that all efforts to facilitate a deaf child's language development will eventually contribute to his ability to learn to read and write.

Notes

1. One method of writing ASL, called *sign-writing,* has been used in a newsletter printed in California and has been developed by Gleaves and Sutton into a software program called Sign-Writer 4.4. This shareware enables the typing of symbols without using the mouse and permits the changing of symbol variations without lifting the fingers from the keyboard.

2. Sign-stream, a computerized multimedia database tool developed at Boston University, may hold some promise for analyzing ASL captured on video, because facial expression, body language, movement, space, and other linguistic features can also be examined along with the signs.

CHAPTER 3

An Auditory Link to Language

This chapter will help you understand

- How deaf children differ from each other with respect to residual hearing
- The use of hearing aids and assistive listening devices
- The supplementing of audition through speechreading, Cued Speech, Visual Phonics, and tactile devices
- The potential benefits and limitations of cochlear implants

---

Years ago, Mary placed her son, John, in a shopping cart and entered the supermarket through the automatic door only to be confronted by two elderly women, one of whom asked Mary, "Why did you put a Walkman on such a young child?" Mary paused, momentarily taken aback by this unexpected inquiry, then replied, "That's no Walkman. They are a special kind of hearing aid called auditory trainers. My son is deaf. He uses these hearing aids at school, but this afternoon we're experimenting with them outside of school." Today, most hearing aids (and auditory trainers) are much smaller than when John was a child, and they look just like the behind-the-ear models commonly worn by deaf and hard of hearing adults.

Mary remembered her first visit to the ear specialist and the audiologist. Her baby had been at-risk because she had contracted maternal rubella in the second month of her pregnancy. The professionals had each explained to her how the ear works. They told her that sounds travel through the air as waves, which go down the ear canal and vibrate the eardrum. This, in turn, causes fluid in the cochlea in the inner ear to move and the hair cells to bend, which produces electrical impulses. These impulses are then transmitted to the auditory nerve and on up to the brain, where they are interpreted as sound. In the case of her son, John, Electric Response Audiometry (ERA)—a form of electrophysiological testing—showed that although he was deaf, he could hear some sounds. Mary learned that deafness was not an all-or-none phenomenon and that no two children have the same degree of hearing loss. In fact, deafness can range from a condition so slight that it can barely be noticed to an almost total loss of auditory function in one or both ears.

When John started school, Mary also learned that there is a critical link between communication and literacy. Invariably, successful readers had parents who had made communication a major centerpiece of their efforts to raise a deaf child. If parents chose to use signs then they made an all-out effort to learn to sign in order to ensure that their child had access to signed communication at home. Mary decided that speech would be best for John, so she began to do all that she could do to make sure that he was fitted with hearing aids that helped him and that he received numerous opportunities to learn how to use them, such as the aforementioned shopping trip.

A Description of Hearing Loss

Audiological data derived from tests are usually summarized and presented in a format that laypeople can readily understand. For example, we can determine the average hearing level of a person by measuring the softest tones that can be heard in the better ear at 500, 1,000, and 2,000 Hertz (Hz). Middle C on the piano is at 256 Hz. These results are then added and divided by three, and the average hearing threshold levels (HTL) that are obtained can then be arranged in categories.

Average HTL	Degree of Loss
0–15 decibels	Within normal levels
15–24	Slight
25–39	Mild
40–54	Moderate
55–69	Moderately severe
70–89	Severe
90+	Profound

John's hearing loss was caused by damage to the nerve cells in his inner ear, a condition called *sensory neural loss*. This is, by far, the most common form of hearing loss. Another type—*conductive hearing loss*—occurs when the middle ear is obstructed or malfunctions to the point that sound is not adequately transmitted to the inner ear. John's hearing threshold at 500 Hz was 60 dB, at 1,000 Hz was 65 dB, and at 2,000 Hz was 70 dB. Adding 60, 65, and 70 and then dividing by 3 gives 65 dB. So John would be classified as having a moderately severe hearing loss.

These categories, however, are nothing more than an ungainly attempt to summarize a child's audiogram (a graph of what is heard), and they provide only a rough guide to a child's future development. To be a successful hearing aid user, every child must have the following:

• Consistent use of appropriate hearing aids from an early age
• Opportunities to receive a great deal of language under good acoustic conditions
• Many interactions in social settings that will help with comprehension

When these conditions are met, then the following expectations (which are only estimates and will not apply to all children with a hearing loss) may occur:

• With a HTL of 55–69 dB and no additional disability, children such as John can be expected to develop language with the use of hearing aids. Usually they will be able to attain their education in a local school setting but may require an FM (frequency modulated) system or some other auditory training device to overcome extraneous noise. Likely, they will need support services, such as a visiting teacher of deaf children, to monitor their language development and the extent of their social engagement with peers. Speechreading may help in their communication, but hearing aids will usually enable them to partially or fully understand the radio, talk on the telephone, and understand, to some extent, speech on TV. People with this degree of hearing loss are typically referred to as being hard of hearing.

- Children with a HTL of 70–89 dB (severe), in addition to hearing aids and informed parents, will probably need additional help, such as specialized instruction from a teacher of deaf children. Speechreading may help when noisy environments are distracting a child, but signing becomes an appealing option for many children in the upper range of this category (HTL of 80 dB and above). Thus, children who fall in this category can be referred to either as hard of hearing or deaf, depending upon which modality they use for communication—speech or sign.

- Children with a HTL of 90+ (profound) will most likely need supplementary input through another sense, such as vision. If the parents want this child to communicate orally then, in addition to hearing aids, he may have to rely a great deal on his ability to speechread, which, as we shall see, is no simple task. On the other hand, the parents might want an alternative form of visual communication that is less confusing, such as signing. Children with this degree of hearing loss are typically referred to as being deaf.

But the above information relating to categories of hearing loss is still an inadequate picture because there are many factors that can impact on how well a child learns to communicate and eventually become literate. These factors include cause of deafness, age at onset of deafness, age at diagnosis (the earlier the better!), the presence of additional disabilities, and aptitude and motivation for learning. Age at the onset of deafness is very important because a hearing loss can occur before, during, or after a child is born—sometimes years later. Children who become deaf before they acquire language (prelingually deaf) will be linguistically quite different from a child who is deafened after he has acquired language (postlingually deaf).

For these reasons and many others, there can be no "typical deaf child." Each deaf child is unique. Nor is there one particular road that all deaf children must travel to acquire language skills. But one thing is certain: Deaf children need to communicate because it is only through effective communication, which leads to literacy, that they will be able to learn, work, contribute to society, and enjoy a fulfilling life.

The two most common means of communication used with deaf children are signing and speaking. They can be used together or they can be used separately, and sorting out which approach should prevail for a particular child can only be resolved by examining carefully the many variables involved.

Hearing Aids and the Use of Residual Hearing

For those deaf people who can gain some benefit from the use of electronic devices that amplify sounds, the most common appliance is the hearing aid, which works somewhat like a telephone. It converts sound into electrical energy, amplifies that energy, and changes it back into sound. This amplification makes speech louder but does not necessarily make it clearer or more understandable. Although some deaf children can use hearing aids to discriminate speech sounds or become aware of some differences among speech sounds, there are others who benefit very little from amplification. Each deaf child is different. For example, the amount of residual hearing (or conversely, the degree of hearing loss) varies for each child, and this will greatly affect his ability to benefit from amplification. Among the other variables that modify the optimum use of a hearing aid are the type of hearing loss, the age at onset of deafness, the extent of damage to the auditory system, the age at which the hearing loss was diagnosed, and the age when the hearing aids were fitted.

It is important to understand what a hearing aid can and cannot do. No hearing aid will ever enable a child to hear as well as he would if he did not have a hearing loss, because it cannot totally compensate for the hearing loss. Some limits are imposed by the damage to the ear, others by the nature of speech sounds, and still others by the electroacoustic limitations of the hearing aid itself.

There are many different types of hearing aids, and they vary in size, cost, and efficiency. The basic hearing aid can be described as a personal, wearable, public address system. It has a microphone, an amplifier, a speaker, a source of power (a small battery), and a custom-made earmold to couple the speaker to the ear. This hearing aid amplifies all sounds in the environment, but not every sound gets the same amount of amplification. Some low-frequency sounds might receive little amplification, whereas middle- to high-frequency sounds might receive more. This characteristic of different levels of amplification at different frequencies is referred to as the frequency response of an aid. The amount of amplification provided when the volume control is fully on is called the "gain" of an aid. The upper limit of the hearing aid's power is the maximum output or saturation-sound-pressure-level, which represents the loudest sound the aid will produce.

All hearing aids need some kind of fine-tuning (such as adjustment with a volume control), automatic gain control, and pliable soft or hard earmolds to provide a seal in the ear canal to prevent feedback. (Note: The term *feedback* applies to the whistling sound that occurs with loose-fitting earmolds. This happens when sounds amplified by the hearing aid are repeatedly picked up by the aid's microphone, amplified, sent to the ear through the earmold, and then picked up again by the microphone.) The earmold and tubing are, however, more than just coupling devices. The shape and size of the bore, or hole, down which the sound travels will affect the quality of what is amplified. Earmolds with a flared, horn-shaped bore that widens out as it enters the ear canal will more effectively transmit high-frequency sounds (at or above 2,000 Hz). As we shall see below, modern hearing aids can be adjusted in a variety of ways to provide additional amplification for particular frequencies. To enable listeners to better hear telephone conversations, a switch is available that can be moved from the microphone or M position to the T position (called the T-switch), so that the hearing aid will pick up electromagnetic signals, and the telephone coils in the aid will convert them back into sound.

There are also special-purpose hearing aids that are generally in use in educational settings and are generically referred to as *auditory trainers*. These include aids that use infrared light to transmit the speaker's voice, speech training units, and group hearing aids. By far, the most important is the FM unit used to help deaf children hear their teachers more effectively from a distance. The unit consists of a radio microphone worn by the teacher and a small receiving unit worn by the child that are usually coupled in some way to the individual hearing aid. FM systems are reliable and not only avoid the reduction in intensity of speech due to distance but also provide a better signal-to-noise ratio, thus allowing for a clearer sound to be transmitted to the ear than is normally possible with hearing aids.

One system for classifying hearing aids is the location on the head where the aid is worn. The four major types in use today are

- Behind-the-ear (BTE)
- In-the-ear (ITE)
- In-the-canal (ITC)
- Completely-in-the-canal style (CIC)

Body aids worn on the torso and eyeglasses aids have all but faded into obsolescence. The most popular choice for children is the BTE aid because ITE aids often have a loud whistling noise, which is caused by the child outgrowing his earmold(s).

Most hearing aids are air-conduction types that amplify sounds into a child's ear canal. But a few children are fitted with a bone conduction aid. This consists of a headband that holds a bone conduction receiver securely to the head at ear level. The bone conductor aid is useful for persons with a conductive loss (in the external or middle ear) or who are unable to wear an earmold because of an absent or unusually formed external canal or because of chronic middle ear problems.

The second method of classification concerns the different circuitry technologies involved. Each of the four types of hearing aids listed above can have one or other of the six technologies that are arranged below in order of electroacoustic sophistication.

- The first and lowest order is the basic hearing aid, which is tuned generally with a small screwdriver to adjust the frequency response, gain, and maximum output for a particular user.
- The next level up is the compression or automatic signaling hearing aid. In practice, compression means that soft sounds will be amplified more than moderate sounds and that very loud sounds will not be amplified at all.
- The third is the computer-programmable compression hearing aid. Here, the audiologist hooks up the hearing aid to a computer, which calculates what the aid should do for a particular user.
- The fourth type is the multiple-channel computer-programmable hearing aid. If a person needs slight amplification for a soft low-frequency sound, no amplification for a loud low-frequency sound, substantial application for a soft high-frequency sound, moderate amplification for a moderately loud high-frequency sound, and slight amplification for a loud high-frequency sound, and, at the same time, needs all very loud sounds kept from becoming uncomfortable and wants as much clarity as possible, then it makes sense to wear this type of hearing aid, which will divide the incoming sound into multiple channels. It has a computer chip that handles the channels separately and independent of each other.
- The fifth type is the multiple-channel, multiple-memory programmable hearing aid. When an audiologist is trying to provide a deaf child with the best possible hearing in both quiet and noisy environments, she can program the computer chip to accommodate numerous acoustic environments. For example, the aid can be programmed to optimize hearing in a restaurant, in a classroom, at home with the TV on, and in the car.
- The sixth, and currently top-of-the-line, hearing aid is the all-digital aid in which the entire circuit is a computer. Sometimes confusion arises over the difference between programmable and

digital aids because they are both often advertised as being digital. Programmable aids are fitted using digital techniques, but a true digital aid contains its own microcompressor that controls daily operation (Dillon 2001).

There is also the question of whether one or two aids should be worn. The superiority of binaural over monaural aids for all but a small minority of children is no longer in doubt. Despite early controversy, the fitting of two separate aids, one to each ear, has, in most cases, been shown to result in better speech discrimination in the presence of background noise as well as in other difficult listening conditions.

There is little doubt that it is much harder to fit hearing aids to children than to adults. In both cases, the audiologist must be aware of the physical and electroacoustic characteristics of the hearing aid and also be able to use the data obtained from the audiometric test results to prescribe optimal amplification over the desired frequency range. These tasks are not without difficulty, and it would be fair to say that the selection of the most appropriate hearing aids—particularly for young children—is still more an art than a science. An adult can respond readily to auditory tests, particularly those that involve speech reception, but young children are not always capable of doing this. Moreover, adults with their well-established language ability can function fairly effectively with hearing aids that would be inadequate for young children who have yet to learn how to communicate.

In summary, for most hard of hearing children and some deaf children, a hearing aid can be a valuable tool, and in some cases, even an indispensable one. But it is doubtful if hearing aids will prove satisfactory in every way, because they will distort sound to some extent, they are prone to feedback at high intensity, they do not always perform well in noisy environments, and young children frequently unintentionally damage them. Because of the different degrees and different types of hearing loss, as well as the other variables mentioned above, there can be no one best hearing aid that will fit everybody. It will remain for a qualified audiologist who has had considerable experience with deaf children to prescribe and fit the most appropriate hearing aids for your child.

Hearing Aid Usage and Children

Beginning hearing aid use with children can sometimes be difficult because the reactions of both parents and children vary so greatly. Some parents feel apprehensive about prostheses and find that placing hearing aids on their child is an almost insurmountable task. Other parents who may not yet have come to terms with their child's deafness can feel uncomfortable or even embarrassed when people see hearing aids on their child. And then again, there are parents who have no difficulty at all in accepting hearing aids for their child. Children also behave differently. Some accept the aids right away, some would prefer to dump their hearing aids into the toilet bowl, and there are a few who actually go ahead and do that.

The major aim of amplification is to get deaf children to develop auditory comprehension. The emphasis is not so much on teaching them how to hear but on giving them a reason to listen, so that they can learn how to extract meaning from the language that surrounds them in everyday life. Deaf children with sufficient residual hearing and well-fitted hearing aids who have direct exposure to spoken language on as many occasions as possible will be helped considerably. Unfortunately, our natural instinct is to talk less to a child who is deaf, because we figure that he can't hear us so why bother, whereas the complete opposite is required if aided hearing is to be used to the greatest advantage.

With respect to comprehension, deaf children who use hearing aids are most likely to learn a spoken language such as English if they are exposed to a lot of that language in situations that allow them to deduce the meaning of what is said. There are at least four stages through which speech patterns are processed, including,

- Detection: Knowing that speech is present but not recognizable
- Discrimination: Recognizing a word within a closed set, such as when an older child discriminates between *ship* and *sip* or *chew* and *shoe*

- Identification: Identifying a word amongst an unlimited number of items
- Comprehension: Understanding a message

Very young deaf children (less than six months) will often accept the hearing aids better than older children; even so, parents sometimes have to become ingenious to keep the aids on small heads. Generally, the audiologist (and other parents) will share helpful ideas, such as using a bonnet, headband, plastic ring, and various types of straps and tapes. Alterations to the tubing and the possibility of mini-aids can also be investigated.

When hearing aids are selected, it is crucial that they provide optimal amplification over the frequency range of speech, especially for the high-pitch sounds, such as *s* and *sh;* and if possible, amplified speech should not be distorted. The next generation of hearing aids for children will most likely be digital and more sophisticated instruments than their more conventional predecessors. Ongoing research will no doubt determine what the advantages are for children with varying degrees of residual hearing.

Assistive Listening Devices

Assistive listening devices (ALDs) are amplification systems designed specifically to help people hear well in a variety of listening conditions. ALDs can be used with a personal hearing aid or by themselves. Their basic purpose is to improve the signal-to-noise ratio for the listener and to overcome problems due to distance from the sound source. They can be used in large public facilities, small groups, or individual situations for the enjoyment of TV, stereo, and conversation. Four common types of ALDs are presented below.

Personal Amplified Systems

Personal amplified systems are pocket-sized units that can be used indoors and outdoors. They can be used with earphones, headphones, neckloops, or telecoil couplers. The basic unit is a personal amplifier, but some systems use optional modules that enable the unit to be used as a receiver for FM, infrared, or both types of transmissions.

Infrared Systems

An infrared system transmits sounds by light beams, and these sounds can't spill over to other rooms. For this reason, multiplex theaters are often equipped with such systems. However, they cannot be used outdoors because of interference from sunlight. (Interference can also occur from bright incandescent lights.) The system is relatively easy to set up and is ideal for TV listening and small group meetings.

FM Systems

FM systems transmit sound by radio waves (generally on 72- to 76-MHz frequencies). The speaker wears a miniature transmitter and a microphone and the listener uses a portable receiver with earphones. In many instances, the receiver can be coupled to the individual hearing aid. If multiple FM systems are used in rooms that are physically close together, separate broadcast frequencies must be used because FM signals are not limited to line of sight, and can penetrate walls and ceilings, spilling over into other close-by areas. FM systems are commonly used in schools.

Loop Systems

Loop systems consist of a wire loop placed around a listening area and connected to an amplifier and microphone used by the person who is speaking. Speech signals are amplified and circulated through the loop. Telecoil-equipped hearing aids and special receivers can be used to pick up electromagnetic signals and convert them back into sound. Again, the system is easy to install and, in spite of spillover, can be used for small meetings, TV, or even in automobiles.

Deaf people also use many other aids to help them with communication in their daily lives. A hearing ear dog is trained to alert its master to specific sounds, such as alarms, doorbells, telephone rings, crying babies, and so forth. Electronic devices are also available to convert sound signals into strobe lights or vibrations that act as signaling systems for wake-up calls, telephones or text telephones (TTYs), smoke detectors, and fire alarms.

Deaf people can make and receive telephone calls by using a TTY, which consists of a portable teletypewriter connected to a phone by a special adapter. The person receiving the call must also have a TTY, which types out the message that was sent. When a TTY is not available (as is the general case for hearing persons), a message relay center (MRC) can be used, where messages are relayed back and forth by a hearing person acting as intermediary. In the United States, a person can dial 711 in any state to reach an MRC. In other situations, deaf people sometimes use an inter-writer who uses a headset to listen and speak on the phone and signs what is being said to the deaf person.

Deaf people also enjoy television through the widespread use of closed captioning, and the advent of the computer has made possible the use of stenographers or typists who relay messages by typing all that is being said onto a computer screen that can then be read. The future holds much promise for the transmission of information in a visible form by converting speech into writing or by sending live pictures using TV videophones.

Supplementing Audition

When aided hearing gives inadequate sensory information, vision and touch can be used, but these senses are generally not as effective as hearing in receiving speech signals.

Speechreading

The ability to watch the movements of a person's lips, jaw, and tongue as well as facial expression and body movement in order to understand what is being said is now called *speechreading* and not *lipreading,* because more than just the lips are involved. There are some deaf people who can speechread remarkably well, but there are also others with similar visual acuity, language levels, and intelligence who find this skill almost impossible to master. The reasons for this have yet to be isolated.

Speech consists of elements that differ from each other in the way they sound and yet do not always differ in the way they look on the lips. Only 30 percent of all English words are distinguishable by reading the lips alone. Some of these are homophones (words that sound the same, such as *would, wood; to, two, too; whale, wail*) that look alike on the lips. Others sound completely different but cannot be distinguished by reading the lips (*bat, ban, bad; rat, ran*). The information provided by speechreading, therefore, can be fragmentary and confusing.

In addition, the components of speech that we can see specify only part of the message. Little if any information is available on prosody (intonation and stress) or suprasegmental aspects (intensity, frequency, and duration of voice). Moreover, some sounds are invisible (/k/, /g/, /ng/), other sounds are easily confused, such as adjacent vowels (*head/had; dip/deep*). More troubling, all the voiced-voiceless pairs cannot be distinguished on the lips. By saying the following words in front of a mirror and watching the lips the reader will readily observe that the words within each group are visually identical: *pat-bat-mat; fan-van; tow-dough-no; sue-zoo; coat-goat; cheap-jeep.* And if this weren't enough, co-articulation (speech movement in words), voicing, and nasality also cannot be observed. Several vowels can also be visually confused because of the similarities in lip spread and rounding.

These difficulties led Erber (1972) to state that speechreading requires a person to receive a forty-phoneme message through a sixteen-viseme system—a task that proves too difficult for many deaf persons. (A viseme is a generic facial image that can be used to describe a particular sound. Visemes are the visual equivalents of phonemes, or unit of sound, in spoken language.) Estimates vary, but it can be readily understood why even an experienced speechreader may be able to identify as little as 20 percent of speech, even in context, and why others will have still much lower scores. Speechreading is, without a doubt, no easy task.

Nonetheless, in spite of these tremendous difficulties, speechreading is used by some deaf children to supplement their hearing ability. The results obtained from using audition (hearing aids) and vision (speechreading) together are usually greater than the sum of the parts. For example, if a child obtains a score of 10 percent in speechreading and 15 percent in hearing, he may score 30 percent or higher when the material is presented simultaneously through both vision and audition rather than the arithmetically expected 25 percent.

Generally, parents and teachers don't set out to teach specific speechreading skills or to provide the child with a series of drills. The best approach for deaf children is to use the dialogue of everyday authentic situations that interest him and that will promote language skills, such as bathing, dressing, playing, and reading. Children will learn the speechreading and auditory skills they need better if they are encouraged to use these senses at the same time as they are acquiring language. The main precautions parents need to take are listed below.

- Speak normally without exaggerated mouth movements.
- Ensure that the face is in a favorable light and the lips are not obscured.
- Arrange contextual guidance (such as holding the object or picture close to the face at the same time as it is being talked about).

In theory, speechreading for profoundly deaf children is a possible alternative for hearing, but in practice, it is a poor option for most of them. For children with more residual hearing, it can be used to supplement hearing but with variable results. There are some deaf children whose hearing loss is so profound that hearing aids produce only vibrations in the ear, and if the parents want them to communicate orally, speechreading will become their primary means of learning how to communicate. To help this very difficult situation, a few attempts have been made to produce electronic devices to supplement speechreading. One of these is a pair of eyeglasses with tiny lights fitted around the edge of the lens that can be detected by peripheral vision and indicate such aspects as voicing, nasality, and frication of speech. Their use as an aid in communication by deaf children, however, has yet to be demonstrated. Perhaps the best visual supplement to speechreading is Cornett's Cued Speech.

Cued Speech

Cued Speech was developed by Cornett (1967) to reduce speechreading's ambiguity by producing a variety of hand cues at the same time as the spoken message. Sounds that look alike on the lips are associated with different hand cues, and hand cues that are alike are associated with different lip shapes. The handshapes by themselves have little meaning and are simply meant to resolve the confusions that exist in speechreading. Four hand positions differentiate between the adjacent vowels that can be confused, and eight configurations are used to indicate those consonants that look the same on the lips. Moving the hand from one vowel to the other cues the diphthongs. These cues are not difficult to learn, but do take several hours to master, and the practice necessary to become fluent requires considerable time. To get around this drawback, a system of automatic electronic cueing was also developed, but the use of Cued Speech has not become widespread, and so research results are sporadic and do little to promote its future use.

Visual Phonics

A mother of three deaf children designed Visual Phonics, a see-the-sound approach that was then further developed by the International Communication Learning Institute. The system uses forty-three hand cues and corresponding written symbols to help deaf children with their reading and speech. Unlike Cued Speech, where the handshapes and hand positions represent syllables, Visual Phonics represents individual sounds and, in some ways, suggests the sounds they represent. For example, the hand cues for /p/ begin with the hand in a flat position and have the four fingers flick outward quickly like a small explosion. For the long /o/, as in *hope*, the fingerspelled o moves straight and long from the mouth.[1]

Tactile Devices

Speech patterns can not only be heard and seen, they can be felt as well, and electronic devices have been designed to allow touch to be used along with audition and vision as a distant sense. A microphone, amplifier, and receiver pick up the speech signals and vibrate the skin.

The earliest type of vibrotactile device involved a bone conduction vibrator worn on the wrist. Although it failed to make speech intelligible when used in conjunction with speechreading, some very small gains were obtained in speech reception. Next, two-channel services were developed that presented low-frequency sounds to the back of the wrist with one vibrator and high-frequency sounds to the front of the wrist with the other. More recently, a seven-channel device has been produced that is worn around the arm just above the elbow. However, despite design advances over recent years, none has received widespread use.

On the other hand, there are electrotactile devices that present information by delivering an electric current to the skin through small electrodes, and these are proving more efficient than their vibrotactile predecessors. The number of electrodes is variable from a few on the hand to as many as 288 worn on the abdomen to receive the thirty-six bands into which speech is divided. In between these extremes are devices like the Australian "Tickle Talker," which uses eight active electrodes placed below the knuckle on each side of the four fingers on one hand. The microphone is contained in BTE hearing aids, the power source fits into a shirt pocket, and the electrodes are held in place by a mitten-like covering that permits the tops of the fingers to move freely (Blamey and Clark 1985). Tactile devices have shown that they can permit detection, discrimination, and identification of some speech components without other forms of input. Comprehension of running speech through touch alone, however, has yet to be demonstrated. These devices are still in their infancy, and there is some hope that more effective instruments will become available as the research proceeds, but the rate of development is unlikely to be certain, and it may be quite some time before improved models become available.

Cochlear Implants

Hearing aids and most assistive listening devices are used to amplify sound. A cochlear implant is different in that it does not make sound louder but stimulates the surviving auditory nerve fibers in the cochlea, which permits the person to perceive sound. In profoundly deaf individuals, there is generally damage to the cochlea's components that convert sound to nerve impulses, but there may still be some nerve endings that can be stimulated electronically.

Cochlear implants consist of several parts, some worn externally and others surgically placed in the skull or embedded in the cochlea. The major parts of the implant are listed in figure 3.1.

Although there is controversy about implantation in young children, there does exist some broad criteria about who might be a candidate to receive a cochlear implant. It should be noted that these criteria are reviewed and changed as technology and medical techniques improve. Currently, the following candidates may be implanted:

1. Children (twelve months to two years) who are profoundly deaf in both ears and given appropriate intervention have shown a lack of progress in the development of auditory skills
2. Children (two years to seventeen years) with bilateral severe to profound sensorineural deafness who receive little or no benefit from hearing aids
3. Adults (eighteen years and older) with bilateral severe to profound sensorineural deafness and either a pre- or postlingual onset of deafness who receive little or no benefit from hearing aids

People who are deaf as a result of lesions on the acoustic nerve or the central auditory pathway, active middle ear infections, absence of cochlear development, or tympanic membrane perforation in the presence of middle ear disease are not candidates for a cochlear implant. An audiological evaluation and a medical examination, including a high-resolution tomography (CAT) scan of the cochlea,

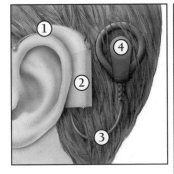
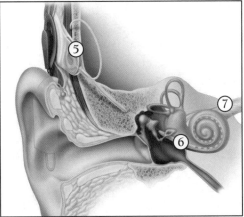

Pictures courtesy of Cochlear Ltd.

The Nucleus® cochlear implant system works in the following manner:

1. Sounds are picked up by the small, directional microphone located in the ear level processor.

2. The speech processor filters, analyzes and digitizes the sound into coded signals.

3. The coded signals are sent from the speech processor to the transmitting coil.

4. The transmitting coil sends the coded signals as FM radio signals to the cochlear implant under the skin.

5. The cochlear implant delivers the appropriate electrical energy to the array of electrodes which has been inserted into the cochlea.

6. The electrodes along the array stimulate the remaining auditory nerve fibers in the cochlea.

7. The resulting electrical sound information is sent through the auditory system to the brain for interpretation.

Figure 3.1. Cochlear implants

form part of the preoperation assessment. The surgery takes several hours but can be conducted as an outpatient procedure.

Some profoundly deaf persons will benefit from an implant, but others may not. Unfortunately, at this time, no one has been able to accurately predict how much, if any, benefit an adult or a child will receive from an implant. Several factors are thought to make a contribution to success. The first is auditory memory. Those subjects who have had some hearing experiences before they became deaf do much better than those who are deaf from birth or became deaf early in life before they acquired language. Second is the status of the cochlea. Individuals with a greater number of nerve fibers will benefit more than others who are not so fortunate. But there is as yet no way to determine the number and location of these residual fibers. It has also been suggested that the age at implementation, the duration of the deafness, motivational factors, and the type of habilitation program will each have some effect on the outcome.

Extravagant claims made by stories in the media have led more than a few parents of deaf children to believe that a cochlear implant provides the user with normal hearing. This is not so. The implant may only provide an awareness of environmental sounds or some speech signal information, and even the best result will provide sounds but not meaning. It is also important to note that the insertion of electrodes into the cochlea will result in a complete destruction of whatever hearing remained in that ear.

Cochlear implants are expensive with costs depending on the person's insurance, health plans, and the charges from the hospital and professionals involved.

With the surgery and general anesthesia required for the transplant, patients are exposed to the normal risks associated with these procedures. In addition, a few adverse side effects have been reported, such as a numbness or stiffness about the ear, injury to the facial nerve, taste disturbances, dizziness, neck pain, and fluid leak from the cochlea. The implant under the skin behind the ear may cause irritation or inflammation. And, in a rare and worst-case scenario, the device extrudes, which may cause the electrode array to migrate partially or completely out of the cochlea. There have also been a few cases where the system failed and had to be replaced. In a public health notification (http://www.fda.gov/cdrh/safety/cochlear.html), the FDA reports a possible association between cochlear implants and the occurrence of bacterial meningitis.

At least fifty-two cases have been diagnosed with ages ranging from twenty-one months to seventy-two years with twelve reported deaths. Most of the cases involved children. At the time of this book's printing, the cause has not yet been established, but the design of the electrode is being considered as a possible factor. Surveys underway suggest that there are additional unreported cases of meningitis in the cochlear implant population.

There are presently three implant devices available in the United States—the Nucleus 24, the Clarion C11, and the MedEl (only the first two are available in Canada). All three have similar components and require similar surgeries, although the number of actual channels varies. The research literature does not point to one device as best, and parents who wish to investigate a cochlear implant for their child should read the material readily supplied by manufacturers, talk to other parents and the families of implant users, check out the availability of services in their location, and carefully consider their relationship with the implant team. Obviously, the implant that best matches with the family and child's needs should be selected.

Learning to understand speech and to monitor his own speech production through a cochlear implant is no easy task for a child, and parents can't just sit back and watch language develop. For children who do not have previously acquired language at least to some extent, it will take several long and arduous years of auditory and verbal therapy to promote spoken language comprehension. It is also important to note that advocates of cochlear implants make the following two assumptions:

1. The earlier deaf children are implanted, the better positioned they will be for acquiring speech and language.
2. The earlier deaf children acquire language, the better chance they will have at becoming literate.

In the process of seeking FDA approval for cochlear implants in children, the Deaf community's viewpoint was not represented. As a result, many Deaf people regard the implant unfavorably.

The World Deaf Federation, for example, is concerned about the invasiveness of the procedure and is most concerned that the outcome for the recipients—especially the quality of life following implantation—still remains unassessed. The federation points out that there has been little or no research into the social or psychological implications of the implant, and has urged investigations into the impact on a child, his family, and peers as well as his self-esteem and sense of identity. Deaf people also maintain that research has yet to show that the procedure improves rather than degrades the quality of life, and they are concerned that potential harm such as marginality is possible. In this situation, the recipient is unable to claim full membership into either the Deaf or the hearing community.

Facilitating the Auditory Link to Language

For young deaf children who are being encouraged to use their residual hearing, the language provided to them should relate to their interests in events and with objects that are part of their everyday experiences. In acquiring language, children both hearing and deaf may not understand the words spoken to them, but they can still grasp the message's intent from the contextual cues available. The social activities that can be used to promote the acquisition of communicative skills, including the expansion of a child's vocabulary, are numerous—eating, dressing, bathing, cooking, cleaning, visiting, shopping, playing, and so forth. For example, at bath time, the parent can say

> We will put water in the bath.
>
> We turn on the taps.
>
> We put the plug in the bath.
>
> We put the washcloth in the water.

As a general rule, the smallest unit of language should be a sentence and not a word because meaning is carried in sentences. There is a linguistic maxim that individual words can be derived from isolated sentences but sentences cannot be derived from isolated words. We would also recommend that parents keep a diary or record of their child's progress. In this way, one can

- Monitor a child's language development
- Analyze the data collected to help in any future decision regarding supplementary and/or alternative language input
- Maintain a list of the concepts that stemmed from everyday social interactions
- Record his journey to the comprehension of language

Finally, regardless of how much benefit deaf children receive from audition, the information they receive visually will always play a critical role in the acquisition of language skills that are needed to become proficient readers and writers. Thus, it is imperative that parents attend to their deaf child's exposure to visual information to which end the next chapter is devoted.

Conclusion

Perhaps the most important tools available in the management of deaf children who are being raised to use speech as their primary means of communication (and this is especially true for those with useful residual hearing) are properly selected and appropriately fitted hearing aids. Because deaf people have different degrees and types of hearing loss, different hearing aids with different adjustments are required to meet individual needs. Digital hearing aids, however, may well overcome the difficulties encountered in earlier selection procedures. Assistive listening devices designed to help deaf people cope with auditory situations include personal amplification systems, infrared, frequency modulation, loop, TTY, captioning procedures, and cochlear implants.

For profoundly deaf children and others who do not receive adequate or sufficient information from amplification, supplements to the auditory signals are available mainly through speechreading and, to a much lesser degree, through the use of Cued Speech, Visual Phonics, and tactile devices. Irrespective of what types of assistive hearing devices deaf children have, all of them need exposure to a great deal of language in situations that enables them to attach meaning to what is being communicated whether it be speech and/or sign and/or script.

Note

1. Further information and materials can be obtained from the International Communication Learning Institute, P.O. Box 39153, Adena, MN, 55439-0153.

CHAPTER 4

A Visual Link to Language

This chapter will help you understand

- How signed communication and other visual communication media can be linked to the printed word
- The importance of exposing deaf children to print in a variety of situations
- The implications of different types of signed communication for literacy development
- Fingerspelling strategies that will help develop a deaf child's comprehension of print
- Strategies for promoting visual information

Audrey's parents were both deaf. They used American Sign Language (ASL) to foster comprehension, but they also exposed their daughter to complete English sentences. Audrey said that the bilingual use of ASL and English in her everyday conversations with her parents made her comfortable early on about using either language. Her father, in particular, relied heavily on fingerspelling to emphasize an English word, phrase, or sentence. Audrey felt that the consistency of her father's signing behavior helped her expand her vocabulary and better recognize patterns in a language. For instance, her father would fingerspell words to show her how base words are used to form other words. Thus, rather than simply signing EXCITE, he would make the sign first and then fingerspell the exact word he needed to express himself precisely in English, such as *excites, excited, exciting, excitedly, excitable, excitability,* or *excitement.* He would also fingerspell whole sentences, and the two of them enjoyed talking

71

about topics that he or Audrey had read in the newspaper or a book. The consistency of this practice helped Audrey recognize these words in print, and this in turn, helped to make the process of learning to read more enjoyable.

Charlene grew up in an oral environment with hearing parents. Her route to reading was through heavy exposure to print in the home. She reported that her mother would have her writing and reading words for thirty minutes each day before school. Starting when Charlene was five years old, her mother would label objects around the house. Charlene's task was to go from one object to another and copy the words down. This activity was followed up with another "matching game" where she placed the card with the name of the object on or beside the actual article in the house. Charlene believed that this helped her develop an association between print and real objects. As she became familiar with these activities, she moved on from single words (such as *fork, table, blind*) to determiner-adjective-noun phrases (*the blue cushion, the empty pot*) to descriptive phrases with prepositions (*the rug under the table in the living room*) and eventually to more abstract tasks that involved a paragraph about something she had done or something she was thinking about.

Many successful deaf readers tell stories similar to those of Audrey and Charlene. Whereas the primary means of communication—signing, speech, and fingerspelling—may change from one success story to the next, common themes are woven throughout each of these stories, including the following:

- The importance of visual information in opening the doors to reading
- The practice of making connections between how a deaf child communicates and the printed word
- The use of consistency and repetition in the linguistic activities that a parent shares with the deaf child
- The importance of authentic interactions between the deaf child and the parent
- The encouragement of the deaf child to read
- The expectancy that the deaf child will read

Deaf children need support in internalizing visual information. In this chapter, we offer four basic principles that can guide your interactions with your deaf child and help you encourage them to use visual information to enhance their communication skills.

Become Effective Communicators

Parents should seek to be clear and expressive regardless of the form of communication from the moment they begin to interact with their deaf child. As a parent, you can do this by

- Modeling effective communication practices as well as encouraging such practices in your deaf child. In this way, deaf children learn not only the value of effective communication but also that it is the speaker's responsibility to be understood.
- Making sure that your child is able to clearly see all forms of visual communication. When speaking to your deaf child, pay attention to the ways by which you express visual information, such as positioning yourself so that the child has a good view of your face and hands. Remove or modify a distraction, such as a mustache that covers the lips. When signing to a child who is in the process of becoming a fluent signer, use both hands to form signs and articulate each sign clearly. If your child comes to appreciate the importance of clearly expressed signs and/or speech then he is more likely to transfer this importance to the expression of printed information.
- Speaking at your child's level of understanding. Express thoughts that your child can comprehend but communicate at a higher level as well, because children must be exposed to higher-level language in order to learn it. However, when you do this, you may have to rephrase or explain what you have said so that your child better understands the message you are trying to convey.

Bring Visual Information to the Deaf Child's Attention

This covers practices that range from ensuring you have eye contact with a deaf child before communicating to drawing his attention explicitly to an item under discussion. Charlene's mother labeled objects throughout the house and then expected her daughter to copy these labels and later make connections between print and objects. When you are going to talk about something, try and provide visual cues concerning the topic, as demonstrated by the actions of the parent in the following:

- Shows a shopping list to the child. "We are going to the K&T to buy groceries."
- Points outside to the black clouds. "It looks like it will rain this afternoon. We will stay home instead of going to the park. What would you like to do?"
- Picks up his school backpack. "Do you have any homework to do today? I can help you if you want."
- Shows a phone number on a cell phone. "I am going to call Judy's mother to see if she can take you and Judy to the soccer game."
- Points to the dishwasher. "It's your turn to take the dishes out of the dishwasher."
- Writes "The Randall family" on a piece of paper. "The Randalls will be coming today at 5:00. Please make sure your bedroom is clean and that you have put away your toys."
- Places a *TV Guide* in front of the deaf child. "What show would you like to watch this evening?"
- Sits the baby sister in front of the deaf child. "I have to leave the house for one hour (points to watch), and I want you to take care of your baby sister for me."
- Points to a box of Lego bricks. "You can play Legos with her if you would like to."

Attach Meaning to Objects and Actions

This principle ties in with building up the deaf child's vocabulary and giving him opportunities to use language to internalize his thoughts about the environment. It also helps him when he needs to draw on his past experiences so that he can better understand the context of something that is in print. For example, the sentence "The bus driver was in a traffic jam caused by a bottleneck on the freeway," will be more readily understood if the deaf child knows what *traffic jam* means and the special characteristics of a *bottleneck* traffic jam. In this instance, you may want to use an actual pop bottle: identify the bottle's neck, explain how the pop has to pass through a narrow opening to leave the bottle, and then draw this analogy to a traffic jam. The best opportunity to teach the meaning of new terminology is to introduce the words in situations where they will have the best chance of being understood. Thus, for the above words, mention them when you are both in a car stuck with a lot of other slow-moving vehicles (i.e., a traffic jam) or when several lanes of traffic are narrowing down to fewer lanes leading to a halting or significant slowing down of traffic (i.e., a bottleneck). If you make a conscious effort to do this, you will be surprised at how many opportunities for vocabulary expansion occur during everyday activities. This procedure will also help provide a visual context for the recognition of words that deaf children might encounter in print.

A good way to help your deaf child internalize his thoughts about his environment is to share your own thoughts about things. In this way, you are modeling how you use language to think about things. You can do this by offering your opinion about things throughout the day.

> The softness of this plum tells me that it is perfectly ripe. I'll bet it tastes sweet. Feel it, then taste it, and tell me what you think.

> Oh, we can't walk on the sidewalk barefoot today. Why do you think the sidewalk is so hot? It is never this hot when it is cloudy or raining.

Link a Deaf Child's Knowledge about Communication to the Printed Word

By *communication*, we are referring to sign and/or spoken communication. In one respect, it could be argued that this principle reflects what teachers have been trying to do with deaf children since the beginning of formal education almost two hundred years ago.

However, what has been neglected in the past is the quality time that parents could have devoted to a variety of communicative acts in print with their child, such as the following:

- In a restaurant. You first write the sentence "Are you thinking about having chicken fingers or pizza for lunch today?" Then you should show it to the deaf child and sign or speak the sentence. Show the sentence to the deaf child again, and ask the child to read or describe (e.g., in ASL) what is written. If you think that such an activity might be tiresome to a deaf child, consider the fact that hearing families don't direct a lot of communication to a deaf child. The practice of writing the occasional sentence that has been signed or spoken might, in fact, be a welcomed respite from the tediousness of not knowing what other people around the table are saying.
- Watching television. You might ask the question, "What do you think this commercial is about?" or "What do you think Arthur is thinking about?" or "Why do you think this woman lives in a huge mansion?" Or you might say something about what you are watching, such as "The woman in the picture is going for a long run" or "I would love to visit Egypt and sail down the Nile River." Then write the question or statement on a piece of paper and show it to your deaf child. It takes minimum effort to keep a writing pad and a pen by the TV. If you just write two sentences a day, that adds up to fourteen sentences in one week and 728 sentences over the course of a year. If you had been doing this for the past year, do you think it would have helped your deaf child make some connections between signing (or speaking) and print?
- While shopping. Shopping gives you numerous opportunities for introducing new vocabulary and engaging in dialogue that covers many everyday phrases: "Do you need a new pair of blue jeans?" or "Which store do you want to go to now?" or "I didn't bring enough money to pay for the garden tools so I will have to use my credit card." The potency of talking and writing while shopping is optimal because the context is varied, the child's curiosity is usu-

ally piqued, and for many, shopping is a fun activity. You can use these assets to expose your deaf child to phrases that are familiar as well as those that you might not normally say to him. Examples of familiar expressions are "We have to leave now," "What kind of clothes do you need for school?" and "Are we done with shopping? Where would you like to go now?" Not-so-common sentences will be those related to the situation in which they occur. Examples are "You got new shoes two months ago. I am not buying you new shoes today," "You may go to the pastry section and find something you want to have for dessert," and "I am tired of walking in this mall. Let's find your sister and go home."

- Running errands. Think about the times you have taken your deaf child along with you to run an errand away from home. Now think about some of things you talked about. Were they related to the errand that you were doing, such as buying something from a hardware store, going to the bank, filling the tank of your car with gas, buying groceries, buying stamps at the post office, buying supplies for gardening around the house, and so forth? Or were your conversations with your deaf child superficial and predictable, examples of which might include "Are you ready to go?" "We will leave soon," and "Stay close to Daddy so you don't get lost." Because of the predictability of a shopping trip, you should be able to write a few sentences on index cards before leaving your house. This might make it easier for you to engage in this activity and give you the opportunity to think through some sentences that range from linguistically easy to challenging.

The Signing Link

Signing is a visual-spatial form of communication. It is visual because you have to see it to understand it and spatial because the information conveyed is in the space around the signer. It is also gestural because you have to use your hands to express it. There are several forms of signing, all of which can be generically referred to as signed communication. Specific types of signed communication include ASL, English sign systems, and contact signing.[1]

ASL is a language that is used in the Deaf community. It has a vocabulary and grammar that have features that are both similar and dissimilar to the linguistic features of a spoken language.

English sign systems is a generic term that refers to "any type of signing that follows English word order, from haphazard combinations of fingerspelling and signs to formal systems created specifically for coding English in signs" (Stewart and Luetke-Stahlman 1998, 3). Some types of English signing were created mainly for use in the classroom and for giving parents a method for signing what they are saying in speech. All English sign systems draw heavily on ASL for the bulk of their signs. English sign systems have also been referred to as *manually coded English.* Two widely used variants are Signed English and Signing Exact English.

Another type of English signing is contact signing, which combines the signs and linguistic features of ASL but places the signs in English word order. In the literature, the term *contact signing* has come to replace the name *pidgin signed English* (PSE), an earlier name for the same system.

What Does Signed Communication Look Like?

A comparison of the three main types of signing can be made by examining the way each of them conveys the English sentence, "The parade will be cancelled if it rains tomorrow."

In English grammatical terms, this is called a conditional sentence because the cancellation of the parade is conditional (or dependent) upon it raining tomorrow. In the examples below, we will follow the common practice of indicating all signs in small capital letters and hyphenating the letters if the word is fingerspelled. More in-depth descriptions of the features of ASL and other types of signed communication can be found elsewhere. Parents who are considering the use of signs or who are already signing should learn as much as possible about all three types of signing. They should also periodically review their use of signs to ensure that the signed communication they are using still matches their language and communication goals for their deaf child. It should be noted that signing is not limited to the Deaf community and the education of deaf children.

Many hearing children and adults are learning ASL as a second language. High schools and universities offer ASL courses to meet foreign language requirements.

American Sign Language

IF TOMORROW RAIN, PARADE CANCEL

In ASL, a condition is typically placed at the beginning of a sentence followed by the condition's outcome (Stewart 1998). Thus, we have

Condition: IF TOMORROW RAIN

Outcome: PARADE CANCEL

Notice how different the ordering of signs is in ASL from the ordering of the words in the English sentence. A summary and examples of four other rules for creating ASL sentences are shown below and were taken from Stewart's (1998) description of basic ASL rules.

1. Topic/Comment: In a simple topic/comment sentence, the topic is described first followed by the comment.

   English: He's happy that he won $3,000,000.

   ASL: HE WON 3 MILLION DOLLARS, HE HAPPY.

2. Tense with time adverbs: The time adverb is placed at the beginning or near the beginning of a sentence.

   English: The sunset was beautiful last night.

   ASL: LAST NIGHT, SUNSET BEAUTIFUL.

3. Simple yes/no questions: In short sentences that ask a yes/no question, the order of the signs is variable.

   English: Do you want to exercise?

   ASL: WANT EXERCISE YOU?
   YOU WANT EXERCISE?

4. Rhetorical questions: In a rhetorical question, the signer asks a question solely to produce an effect and not to seek an answer from another person. Note, however, that the rhetorical question

designation applies to the ASL translation of the English sentence and not to the English sentence itself.

English: I didn't pay attention to the name of the street and got lost.

ASL: ME LOST WHY? NOT PAY-ATTENTION STREET NAME.

There are other ASL rules, but the ones described above illustrate some of the ways that ASL grammar contrasts with English grammar. However, there are times when ASL sentences are similar to English sentences and, as with other languages, there is usually more than one way to translate a sentence from ASL to English and from English to ASL. Facial expressions are another important linguistic feature of ASL. Just as speech relies on inflection and pitch, ASL depends on facial expressions to indicate what a signer is saying. For example, the tilting of the head slightly forward while squeezing the eyebrows is a facial expression that accompanies questions with the words *who, what, why,* and *how many* in them.

English Sign Systems

THE PARADE WILL BE CANCEL+ED IF IT RAIN+S TOMORROW.

In English sign systems, a signer attempts to code in sign what is spoken in English. Thus, there are signs for each English word. If no sign exists for a particular word, the signer fingerspells it. In addition, all English sign systems provide signs for most of the common English suffixes or word endings, plural forms, and past tense markers. Because these are signs added to a base sign, we indicate their use by preceding them with the notation "+."

English sign systems borrow most of their signs from ASL, examples of which include the signs BOOK, LANGUAGE, WALK, WRITE, READ, CANADA, FRUIT, NAME, WITH, and CHANGE. In addition to borrowed signs, English sign systems use initialized signs to a greater degree than ASL. An initialized sign is formed by using the handshape of the first letter of the sign. In ASL, the handshape for TREE and FOREST is an open hand, which refers to a tree's branches and not the spelling of either word. The ASL sign for FOREST is distinguished from TREE when the signer moves the arm and hand to the side to show that there are many trees.

In Signing Exact English, the sign TREE is made in the same way as it is in ASL. However, FOREST is made with an F handshape. Similarly, ORCHARD is made with an O handshape, and WOODS is made with a W handshape. All of these signs look similar to the ASL sign TREE, except that the handshape represents the manual alphabet for the first letter of each word. Although ASL uses initialized signs to some extent, English sign systems, especially Signing Exact English, use the process of initialization to a much greater degree and place greater importance on the benefits of initializing signs to aid deaf children in their acquisition of new vocabulary.

When there is no readily available ASL sign, English sign systems also often invent signs by using the process of initialization. ASL users, on the other hand, tend to resort to fingerspelling words for which there are no signs. Examples of invented signs that owe their origin to Signing Exact English are FIG, GUINEA PIG, and FREAK (Gustason, Pfetzing, and Zawolkow 1980). In Signed English, invented signs include INCREDIBLE HULK and MAGIC MARKER (Bornstein, Saulnier, and Hamilton 1983.) The link between invented signs and literacy has been described as follows:

> [A]dding new signs to represent specific words helps to increase students' vocabulary. If young children are going to have access to the vocabulary needed to understand social studies and science and to read and write effectively, sign invention is necessary. (Luetke-Stahlman 1998, 25)

In the 1970s, when English sign systems were created for use in the classroom as a model for English, they were intended to be used in conjunction with speech in the belief that signing and speech can complement each other to assist a deaf child's acquisition of English. The use of signs and speech at the same time is called Simultaneous Communication. Formal English sign systems, such as Signed English and Signing Exact English, were never meant to be used alone without speech and were never meant to replace ASL as an effective means of communicating. Instead, through the use of Simultaneous

Communication, it was felt that deaf children would be able to gain information from both the speech modality and the sign modality, which, in theory, would lead to an overall improvement in comprehension. The jury is still out as to the extent to which exposure to English in signs translates into the ability to read and write in English.

All the English sign systems also have specific rules that apply to them. For instance, Signing Exact English uses a two-out-of-three rule with respect to a word's spelling, meaning, and sound. If two words match on any two of these three aspects then these words will share the same sign. The word *bread* in the following sentences will have the same sign because, although the meaning is different, it is spelled the same and sounds the same in both sentences:

We need a loaf of bread for lunch.

I'm broke can you lend me some bread?

Contact Signing

PARADE WILL CANCEL I-F RAIN TOMORROW.

PARADE WILL B-E CANCEL I-F RAIN TOMORROW.

T-H-E PARADE WILL CANCEL I-F RAIN TOMORROW.

These sentences represent just three examples of how contact signing renders an English sentence into signs. Further examples of contact signing can be created by signing more or less of the English sentence. The following are the central features of the three sentences above:

1. Each one follows the original ordering of words in the English sentence.
2. Each sentence is marked by a reduction in the amount of English morphemes and grammar that is signed.
3. ASL signs are used.
4. The sentences incorporate one of ASL's linguistic features—the absence of any direct indicator of the third person singular for the word *rains.*

Contact signing is the type of signing that teachers of deaf children commonly use in their classroom. Because of the reduction of English grammatical structures, contact signing is easier to use when the person is also speaking at the same time (i.e., using Simultaneous Communication). With contact signing, a person can speak in complete English sentences yet not sign each word in the sentence.

Contact signing is also prevalent in the Deaf community. In fact, some people believe that contact signing is a variation of ASL (but we are not going to pursue that argument in this context). Our intent is to provide a simple illustration of the three types of signing to give you a template for examining your own signing behavior or to help you decide on the type of signing you may wish to use with your deaf child.

Signed Communication and Literacy Development

What are the implications that signed communication has for literacy development? Deaf children who use signs are typically exposed to both ASL and English and are therefore living and learning in a bilingual environment. This is also true for deaf children who attend a school program that uses an English sign system. Research has shown that even though the teachers in these programs may be strict in their use of an English sign system, their students tend to use ASL or contact signing with each other.

ASL/English Bilingual Programs

Different ASL/English bilingual approaches have been developed that revolve around the nature of how each language is used to enhance communication. Two common programs are distinguished by the approach they use in teaching English literacy.

1. ASL is the primary language for interacting with others inside and outside of the classroom; English is used only in reading and writing activities. Proponents of this approach believe that complete forms of English cannot be adequately coded in signs, and therefore signing should not be used to expose deaf children to

English. In this approach, print becomes the primary vehicle
through which deaf children learn English. There is also a heavy
emphasis on incorporating information about Deaf culture—
how Deaf people live and the activities of the Deaf community—
into the curriculum. Programs that have adopted this approach
are called bilingual-bicultural programs or simply "Bi-Bi."

2. ASL and English types of signing complement one another, and
signing supplements the teaching of English through reading and
writing activities. In these programs, deaf children are exposed to
both types of signing. Print is still a vehicle for teaching English,
but English signing is also used. These types of ASL/English
bilingual programs tend to use contact signing as the model for
English signing. Within this type of bilingual approach, the two
languages may be used together in many different ways. For example, parents might use English signing as their major means of
communication but switch over to ASL whenever they feel that
such a change would assist their deaf child's comprehension. Or
they might use ASL most of the time but include English signing
when they want to emphasize certain English sentence structures, read a passage from a newspaper, or quote what someone
had said, and so forth.

Because there has been an insignificant amount of research in this
area, there is little to indicate which is the better approach, although
we can say that deaf children's acquisition of ASL and signed communication in general facilitates their progress to literacy. Some
authors have attempted to circumvent this lack of ASL/English bilin-
gualism research by drawing a comparison with how hearing children learn in bilingual environments. English-speaking children
learning French in Ontario and Spanish-speaking children learning
English in California are two widely studied populations of bilingual children. However, there is a major drawback in drawing con-
clusions for deaf children based on research on hearing children—
ASL does not have a written component. Thus, the transfer of the
alphabetic knowledge of one language to another language, such as
occurs with hearing bilingual children, does not take place with deaf

children. This is a significant consideration for the ASL/English bilingual child because "knowledge of the alphabet system assists in the development of rapid word identification skills" (Paul 1998, 177).

In other words, when a deaf child who is proficient in the use of ASL begins to learn English, which ASL language skills can assist in this learning process? The connection between ASL and English literacy becomes apparent when we view literacy in terms that go beyond notions of reading and writing. When one considers that the development of literate thought is related to a deaf child's "ability to think critically and reflectively" (Paul 1998, 178), then the ability to use language—any language—to think and communicate becomes critical.

Implications of Signing for the Development of Literacy Skills

Listed below are connections between the use of signing and literacy development.

Allows Communication

Signing gives deaf children an opportunity to acquire communication skills that can help in learning to read and write. Deaf children who are proficient in their use of signing are better prepared to use print as a medium for improving English skills. Signing allows them to talk and learn about things, and their ability to speak about what they know together with what they learn in their day-to-day activities are crucial elements of the literate mind. Deaf children cannot wait until they can read and write before learning to talk to other people. Signing is therefore a realistic and suitable option for deaf children.

Early Acquisition of Signing

The early development of signing skills facilitates the acquisition of English literacy skills. If signing is going to become a cornerstone of a deaf child's communication then he should learn it from as early an age as possible. In this respect, most teachers of deaf children will agree that profoundly deaf children are able to acquire ASL at an earlier age than English, including English signing. The reason for this is that ASL is a visually based language that can best be learned through seeing. English is an auditory-based language and is best learned through hearing. For deaf children who do not have adequate access to communication through hearing, the ability to learn English in this manner is severely hampered.

This also means that parents should learn to sign while their deaf child is young—and the earlier the better. Deaf parents begin signing to their deaf children from birth, and by the time these children are three years old, they have already acquired a strong command of a language, which they can use to internalize their experiences and, in turn, acquire even more language. Two Deaf parents described their child's language growth as follows:

> When our daughter, Bridget, came into this world, we greeted her with awe—and language. Bridget, like us, is Deaf. From those first wonderful moments in the hospital, we signed and fingerspelled to her. Perhaps because of all this language, she was an alert baby and we introduced her to books quickly. At 34 months old, she had been entertained by over 200 books, an average of four books a day. (Berrigan and Berrigan 2000, 7)

You may feel intimidated by the fact that Deaf parents are already fluent in ASL and are able to start signing to their children (deaf and hearing) from birth. Although this is true, research has shown that when hearing parents learn to sign while their child is still very young, their deaf child can perform as well academically as Deaf children of Deaf parents.

The opportunities to learn to sign, and especially to learn ASL, are constantly expanding. For example, parents can learn ASL through coursework at local colleges, community education programs, or mini-courses offered by their deaf child's school program; through numerous ASL books that are readily available through the Internet (see http://www.amazon.com for a comprehensive listing of books on ASL and English sign systems); through videos; and even through an Internet-based ASL course (see http://www.signingonline.com).

Helps English Comprehension

Signing can be used to facilitate comprehension of what is said or written in English. This point relates to the first point above in that parents who are skilled in ASL can use it to help their deaf child understand something that he has seen in English. This notion is important when introducing deaf children to the pleasures of reading. For example, a mother reads a story in a book to herself, tells the story in signs to her deaf child, and then reads the book again to him. As long as the child understands signing, then a parent can always use signing to aid the child's understanding of written information.

Metalinguistic Awareness

Signing helps deaf children think about language. Thinking about how you use language is called metalinguistic awareness. All children and adults do this. We are constantly thinking about the words we are going to use or the ones we have just used. The way in which this can occur is shown in the following passage:

> A child who has been directed to find the word *cat* responds by pointing to the letter *c* in *cat* and *cookie*, indicating that they are the same. The child's response demonstrates interest in developing the metalinguistic understanding of *letter* and *word*. (McAnally, Rose, and Quigley 1998, 51)

When anyone engages in thinking about how he uses language, he also promotes his own language development. Because signing helps a deaf child think about language in the form of signed communication, we believe it can become a tool for helping him think about language in print.

Fingerspelling

Fingerspelling is an important way to link signing with print. The early use of fingerspelling in all types of signed communication will introduce deaf children to the concept that letters can be joined to form words that have meaning. Extensive use of fingerspelling can contribute to vocabulary growth and provide a means for modeling English grammar. For instance, teachers who use ASL will use fingerspelling "when conveying words that do not have an equivalent ASL sign" (Bailes 2001, 160). Because of its importance in literacy development, the following separate section is devoted to this topic.

Fingerspelling and Literacy Development

Fingerspelling provides a link to English vocabulary in several respects. First, there is the obvious connection with the twenty-six distinct handshapes used to represent the letters of the alphabet (see figure 4.1 for illustrations of the manual alphabet). Using the manual alphabet, every word in English can be fingerspelled; many Deaf adults use their fingerspelling skill to spell out entire phrases and sentences. This technique serves various purposes, including the opportunity

- To express verbatim what was said in English
- To communicate proper nouns such as the names of people and places (e.g., Mt. Rushmore, Sears Tower)
- To express common phrases (*cop out*) and idioms (*The cat is out of the bag*)
- To allow emphasis to be placed on key words
- To introduce new vocabulary
- To spell the English equivalent of a sign
- To say something in secret to someone outside the view of others
- To say something to another person whose knowledge of signs is limited

Deaf children who are exposed to fingerspelling learn at least three important concepts related to emerging literacy. They learn that (a) letters can be put together to form words; (b) these words have meaning; and (c) there is a direct correspondence between letters and words that are fingerspelled and those that are printed.

Throughout this book, we have emphasized the importance of fingerspelling in everyday conversations. In this section, we introduce four strategies for linking communication and thinking skills with print, with an emphasis on the use of fingerspelling during reading activities. These strategies can be used in many different

The American Manual Alphabet

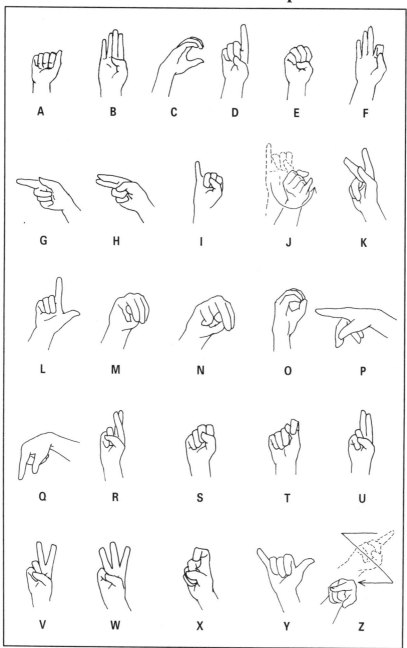

Figure 4.1. The American Manual Alphabet

situations and not just for reading, although Deaf adults have been observed using them when reading to their deaf children.[2] In addition, good teachers use them throughout the day.

Indirect Links to Print

The parent fingerspells and signs the same word or vice-versa. There are also variations of this, such as fingerspelling-signing-fingerspelling or signing-fingerspelling-signing. Whether a word is fingerspelled first or signed first is not as important as the fact that you make an effort to connect the fingerspelling to the word's sign. The words or phrases that are fingerspelled will depend upon what it is that you want your child to notice.

Direct Links to Print

A variation of the above strategy is to show a child the printed word that is being fingerspelled and signed. This can occur in any situation where there is print. A book, flyer, birthday card, cereal box, letter from grandmother, bulletin board, movie ad, and more may all serve as wonderful opportunities to make a connection between print and how a child communicates.

Interactive Links to Print

In this technique, in addition to using a combination of pointing to a printed word, fingerspelling it, and signing it, the parent has the child copy what he has done. For younger children, the parent might

1. Point to a picture (if available)
2. Point to a word
3. Fingerspell the word
4. Sign the word
5. Then ask the child to copy her as she repeats steps 1 to 4

Any variations of these steps would be appropriate as long as the connections are made in a comprehensible and enjoyable way between print, sign, and fingerspelling.

Elaborative Links to Print

In this final strategy, the parent actively engages the child so that he can demonstrate his understanding of what is printed by asking questions that stimulate his thinking about a word in print. These questions should require more than merely a yes/no answer and whenever possible should encourage the child to demonstrate his knowledge of print. For example, for a child who is beginning to recognize words in print, you might ask or give directions

Point to the word D-O-G on this page.

How many times can you see the word G-R-E-E-N on this page?

Sara looks sad in the picture. Can you spell sad? Good for you. Now, can you find the word S-A-D on this page?

As the child's reading improves, you can expand upon the type of questions that you ask and include ones that require the child to read more than one word on a page. Examples of these types of questions are

T-H-E B-I-G T-R-U-C-K. Those words T-H-E B-I-G T-R-U-C-K, where are they on this page?

The father yelled, "COME INSIDE THE HOUSE NOW!" Who is he talking to? He's talking to Bobby, that's right. How do you know that?

S-T-O-N-E S-O-U-P. Wow. Someone wants to make STONE SOUP. I have never eaten STONE S-O-U-P. In the book, who wants to make S-T-O-N-E SOUP?

In this last example, the parent is reading the story "Stone Soup" and deliberately mixes signs and fingerspelling for the words *stone soup*. The parent could also point to the picture of a pot in which stones are being placed and then move ahead to the end of the story where people are eating soup taken from the pot.

An Action Plan for Links to Print Strategies

There are numerous ways in which each of the above strategies can be used. The only limitation is your imagination. Take the following passage from the book *Red Is Best* by Stinson (1982) about a little girl who likes everything red:

> I like my red jacket the best.
>
> My mom says, "You need to wear your blue jacket. It's too cold out for your red jacket."
>
> But how can I be Red Riding Hood in my blue jacket? I like my red jacket the best.

Think about how you might apply one or more of the above strategies. Consider how many times you have already read the book to your child and his understanding of fingerspelling (more about this below) when deciding which strategy to use. You will also have to decide on the words that you want to emphasize. It might be the names of colors, in which case *blue* and *red* will be purposefully fingerspelled. Or you might want to stress the preposition *in* or the entire prepositional phrase *in my blue jacket. Red Riding Hood* is a good one to fingerspell because it appears in many children's books. It is also a proper name, in which case fingerspelling each word is a better choice than signing each one. In each example, you would fingerspell the word, make the sign for the word, point to the word on a page, and/or talk about the word or phrase. Over time, vary the order in which you do these things so that your child is encouraged to learn under a variety of adaptations to a routine.

Given the value of fingerspelling as a link to literacy, it is important for you to make liberal use of fingerspelling when signing. This will mean practicing until you feel comfortable with the manual alphabet—regardless of which type of signed communication you choose to use with your deaf child. There is no rule that one type of signed communication will require more or less fingerspelling than any of the others.

The Deaf Child's Fingerspelling

At some point, you might wonder what to do about your child's accuracy when fingerspelling words. As he gets older, becomes more fluent in signing, and is in the process of becoming an experienced reader, accuracy in fingerspelling becomes more important.

For younger deaf children—emerging signers and emerging readers—accuracy should be allowed to take its own course according to the child's developmental stage. As with writing, poor spellers do not necessarily equate with poor readers. Thus, although we aim for accuracy at some point, our overriding concern is that the child (a) feels comfortable using fingerspelling as a means of talking to people and (b) understands the connection between fingerspelling and print.

Finally, modeling good fingerspelling behavior is an excellent way to teach deaf children the importance of such behavior. Although you should start this at an early age, there is no benchmark as to when a deaf child should be expected to be a "good" fingerspeller. An example of the importance of modeling is shown in the following description of how a Deaf mother and father used fingerspelling to read books about Franklin the turtle to their thirty-month-old Deaf daughter, Bridget:

> We fingerspelled many words as we read this (sic) book to Bridget, including *shell, goose, parachute, supper, bed,* and *franklin.* We fingerspelled the name of Franklin, the turtle star of both books, and Bridget recognized both the fingerspelled and printed name and frequently fingerspelled the word to us. Here's our record of how her fingerspelling evolved over a two-week span.
>
> F-L-N
>
> F-R-L-N-I
>
> F-R-K-L-N-I
>
> F-R-A-N-K-L-N-I
>
> F-R-A-N-K-L-I-N-I
>
> F-R-A-N-K-L-I-N
>
> Just before Bridget's final mastery of Franklin's name, she spelled it with an extraneous I (F-R-A-N-K-L-I-N-I). We never corrected Bridget's

fingerspelling, teaching her instead through modeling. But on one occasion, when she attempted to correct Dennis as he spelled the turtle's name without its phantom ɪ, he offered an explanation. "There's no ɪ at the end of Franklin," he told her. He pointed to the word in the book, and then he fingerspelled it again. Bridget watched intently. The next time she fingerspelled Franklin, the extraneous *I* was gone. (Berrigan and Berrigan 2000, 8–9)

Modeling good fingerspelling behavior is something that all parents should strive to achieve. If you require such behavior of yourself, then your child will come to expect that he should behave in a similar manner. As with Bridget in the passage above, there will be times when you will have to explain why you are doing something; moreover, if you are a parent of an older child, then you will need to explain certain things over and over again. Explanations and modeling make significant contributions to a child's learning, and as long as you persist with these two behaviors, you will be giving your child many opportunities for learning.

Conclusion

As parents, you will want to know how you can use visual information to enhance the literacy skills of your deaf child. Signing is an obvious source of visual information for profoundly deaf children, but so is speech and speechreading when a deaf child is trying to understand another person's speech. Signing receives much attention in the literature and schools because, for most hearing parents, it represents a new and different way of communicating.

Over the past three decades, there has been much discussion about which type of signed communication is the best to use with deaf children. In the absence of any research evidence to the contrary, the one response that we can give is that each type of signed communication can make a significant contribution to the development of a literate mind. A more important consideration should be how can the signs be used to help a deaf child develop an awareness of the importance of effective communication. Signing by itself will not necessarily lead to improved literacy skills, and other visual information needs to supplement each form of signing to help deaf children make the connection between what they sign and the printed word.

This is also true for deaf children who use speech to communicate. Deaf children rarely understand 100 percent of what a person is saying through listening alone. Speechreading and other visual clues, such as those described in this chapter, are necessary to provide support for their attempts at communication.

The development of literacy skills in deaf children can be stimulated when parents make generous use of visual information to link signed and/or speech forms of communication with print. Visual information is a broad term and includes how parents position themselves when communicating with their deaf children, the things they point to, and the use of print itself to facilitate their deaf child's efforts to read. It includes speaking clearly for the benefit of those deaf children who rely on speechreading. For deaf children who use signing, the clear articulation of signs and a heavy use of fingerspelling can both help considerably in promoting literacy development.

Notes

1. Given the wealth of information on the nature of signing, we offer only the briefest of definitions of ASL English signing, and contact signing. For more information, the reader is referred to *The Signing Family: What Every Parent should Know about Sign Communication* by Stewart and Luetke-Stahlman (1998) and *Language in Motion: Exploring the Nature of Signs* by Schein and Stewart (1995).

2. See Blumenthal-Kelly (1995) and Schleper (2000).

CHAPTER 5

It All Begins with Experience

This chapter will help you understand

- The role that everyday experiences play in the development of literacy skills in deaf children
- How frequent and meaningful communication prepares deaf children for reading and writing activities
- How you can plan for meaningful experiences and communication with your deaf child

---

One of the authors of this book is a Deaf professional with a profound hearing loss. He has always said that one of the main reasons he can read and write well was that his parents spent a lot of time doing things with him when he was a child. He learned much from these adventures that helped him relate to the stories and information in the books he read. Here is a list of some of the activities he did as a youngster that he remembers well because of the frequency with which they occurred and the pleasure he derived from them. All took place outside of school activities and were required by his parents.

- Art classes
- Judo
- Lacrosse
- Hockey
- Cooking lessons
- Swimming lessons
- Camping almost every weekend during the summer
- Weddings and funerals

- Visits to the barbershop to watch his Dad get a haircut once a month
- Drama club
- Shopping for groceries and clothes
- Shopping at a lumberyard
- Square dancing
- Picking blueberries, strawberries, and raspberries every year
- Evening or day trips to the beach
- His sister's violin lessons
- Museums
- Visiting family friends
- Day trips to parks and mountains
- A trip once a year to buy a license plate for the car
- Drive-in movie theaters
- Trips to islands on a ferry
- Long family vacations once a year
- Looking at open houses
- Looking at new cars in showrooms and on the lot
- Going to the library

This is just a short list of things that he did regularly throughout his school years. The nature of each of these activities is secondary to the fact that he spent a lot of time with his parents doing things and talking about them. If his mom wanted to buy milk then he walked to the store with her. If his dad wanted a box of screws then they jumped in the car and went to the hardware store together. He had three sisters and all of them had a similar experience-laden childhood.

These experiences helped him pick up new vocabulary, gave him practice in talking about new things, and helped him learn to shape his thoughts in meaningful ways that pleased his parents and the other people with whom he interacted. It also brought him in contact with many people, which gave him more opportunities for learning how to communicate.

A bounty of experiences is something that most good readers share. They use their rich experiential background to help them understand and relate to what an author is saying. A lack of this kind of experiential background often strongly contributes to a deaf child's difficulty in learning to read. For deaf readers, the very act of reading often raises a list of things that they must do in order to comprehend a word, sentence, or passage.

Gaining experiences starts in the home. It starts with parents who encourage their child to see and do things and then talk to him about these activities and adventures. In this chapter, we urge parents to do two things.

1. Expose your deaf child to many experiences by doing things with him.
2. Immerse these experiences in conversations.

All babies enter the world with an ability to talk in speech and in signs—a raw ability that takes time to develop. There are at least two reasons why an infant's ability to learn to communicate is important to discussions about literacy development. First, and our oft-repeated mantra, is that talking in either speech or signs directly contributes to the development of language, and it is through language that children internalize their experiences, observations, thoughts, and feelings.

The second reason is found in the parents' behavior. Hearing parents of deaf children tend to wait too long before taking advantage of the innate ability of infants to learn to communicate. Parents seem to operate under the misunderstanding that until their deaf child is able to sign or speak well, they should not overburden them with language.

This type of thinking, of course, is balderdash. Infants and children thrive in a stimulating environment and, as we saw in the previous chapter, a visual environment is critical for deaf children. Speech sounds or signs alone do not lead to the acquisition of language. They need to be embedded in a communication system that will help them attach meaning to what they see and hear.

Clarke (1983) used the phrase "authentic real world language transactions" (25) for what he described as a key to a deaf child's development of competence in communication. He decried classroom language teaching practices that are divorced from real-world experiences. To him, language is more "than a subject on the curriculum and more than a series of lessons and linguistic exercises" (24). In other words, a deaf child who has been taught to respond to classroom visitors with lines such as "Hello Mrs. Peters. How are you? I am well. I am eight years old" needs to get real. He is saying nothing of significance that will contribute to later growth in literacy skills. Moreover, after hearing a deaf child say these words, Mrs. Peters will be hard-pressed to say something meaningful in return.

Exposure to authentic experiences and conversations that revolve around these experiences are critical in preparing a deaf child for the world of print. It provides him with background information, an expanded vocabulary, and the necessary exposure to the functional use of language. Authentic experiences cover practically all types of experiences (save perhaps, stimulus deprivation). They include everyday experience, the experience of the here and now, the predictable experience, and the experience of the unknown. When these experiences are tied in with conversations, they will contribute to language development and lead to a child having a greater facility with the printed word.

No Easy Way Out: A Word about Conversations

When it comes to being a parent of a deaf child, some hearing parents talk in ways that they normally wouldn't if their child were hearing. This behavior cuts across all types of communication (signing, speaking, and writing) and language (American Sign Language and English). It is also pervasive in all types of environments where parents interact with their child (e.g., home, school, and community). The following three cases illustrate how some parents talk to their deaf child.

Case 1

Mother:	[Speaking to her nine-year-old deaf son] Danny, look who's here. It's Jane's mother, Mrs. Bell. Say hello.
Danny:	Hi.
Mrs. Bell:	Hi Danny. How was school today?
Mother:	She wants to know how school was today.
Danny:	Fine.
Mother:	Danny had a substitute teacher today. The sub was a man who is also deaf. Danny really enjoyed him.

| Mrs. Bell: | That's very nice. |
| Mother: | You can go now, Danny. |

Case 2

Father:	[Speaking to his thirteen-year-old deaf daughter at her school's meet-the-teacher day] This is a nice room Brenda. Show me your desk.
Brenda:	[Shows him the desk]
Father:	Do you like this class?
Brenda:	Yes.
Father:	[Looks over the room then smiles at Brenda] Good. Me too.

Case 3

Sales clerk:	[To the mother of Crystal, a sixteen-year-old deaf girl] Can I help you?
Mother:	Yes, please. I'm looking for a navy blue, knee-length skirt for my daughter. [Turns to Crystal] She's going to help us find you a skirt.
Sales clerk:	We have them in wool and cotton. Which would you like?
Mother:	[To Crystal] She wants to know if you want a wool or cotton skirt. [To the sales clerk] I think cotton would be fine.
Crystal:	It doesn't matter.
Mother:	Okay. We will find something that will look good on you.

The unwritten and likely subconscious rules that underscore the parent's behavior in each of these conversations are

- To minimize the opportunities for the deaf child to engage in meaningful conversations
- To focus the deaf child's communication on something that he expects and has had plenty of practice talking about
- To restrict the amount of time that the deaf child spends communicating
- To control the conversation

Hearing parents would not likely talk to their hearing children in a manner similar to the above examples. In Case 1, a hearing child would have been allowed to talk directly to Mrs. Bell and tell her about his day at school or anything else for that matter. His mother would have assumed the role as a listener as he and Mrs. Bell talked to one another. In Case 2, the father, perhaps in an effort to kill time, might have probed his hearing daughter about a variety of things relating to school such as

Show me the artwork that you were telling me about yesterday.

Who are the people that sit next to you in class?

What classes do you like best, and what classes do you have in this classroom?

Now remember what we talked about on the way here. I am going to ask your teacher about moving you to a different desk because Roy keeps bothering you when you sit in front of him.

In Case 3, it is reasonable to think that the mother would have allowed her hearing daughter to communicate directly with the sales clerk. The mother might have briefly explained to the sales clerk what the daughter was looking for and then asked the daughter to describe the type of skirt that she wanted.

In each of the three cases, the parents are passing up valuable opportunities to use language with their deaf children. It is not always easy to be a model conversationalist, and you should not feel pressed to do this all of the time. But if you make a conscious effort to converse meaningfully with your deaf child in a variety of situations, you will find that it does get easier and the results are very gratifying.

Authentic Experiences Begin in the Home

A long-time teacher of deaf children, Marvin Garretson (1995), calculated that "the actual time spent in the classroom for the average child, whether deaf or hearing, came to just eight percent of the total year" (72). In other words, the time that parents have with their children is far greater than the time their children spend in school. Furthermore, most of the time that parents spend with their children requires little or no planning. Conversations can be anywhere and about anything. They can occur around the dinner table, while hiding and finding objects in the house, while playing "I spy with my little eye," and in many more instances.

Making the Best of Activities at Home or in the Community

Before examining ideas for doing things with your deaf child, we first have a word about watching TV.

> Deaf parents of hearing children were once advised to have the children watch a lot of television. In no case did these children learn English. Without already knowing the language, it is difficult for a child to figure out what the characters in those odd, unresponsive televised worlds are talking about. (Pinker 1994, 278)

Once you have crossed the threshold of not using the TV as your surrogate babysitter, you can spend this time enjoying a conversation with your deaf child in whatever activity you are doing. Stewart and Kluwin (2001) had the following suggestions for parents:

1. *Take your deaf child with you when you are engaged in activities related to everyday living.* He should accompany you when you go shopping for groceries, have a haircut, get an oil change, buy a new faucet for the kitchen sink, see a lawyer, renew your driver's license, go for a walk, talk to your neighbor, and visit the dentist, doctor or the bank.
2. *Involve your deaf child in small jobs that you might normally do yourself.* Your deaf child can help mow the lawn, clean up the garage, put tools away, pull weeds in the garden, clean out the fish tank, . . . clean the dishes, and take clothes to a Goodwill or charity organization.
3. *Go special places with your deaf child.* These are places you go because you enjoy visiting them or because you think they might be an exciting activity. The zoo, art gallery, library, park, mall, theater, and museum are places that many people think about when planning to "do something." But how about going to view open houses that are for sale because they provide a good opportunity to talk about likes and dislikes? Take a trip through the industrial part

of town to show where things are manufactured, food packaged, computers assembled, and items stored in large warehouses.

4. *Play games.* Playing games is an experience, too. Think about books in which the main character is playing a particular game. Understanding what a particular game is about may help your child understand a passage in the book where this game is mentioned.

5. *Check with your child's teacher or with your child to see what is being studied in school and plan an activity that can reinforce this learning at home.* Do you have a child taking tenth-grade biology who is studying plant diversity or a child who is learning about plants in the fourth grade? Either age can benefit from a trip to a horticulture garden, a tree nursery, or a walk through the woods. . . . Is your child studying life in the early eighteenth century? Visit an antique shop to look at furniture from this period. (329–31)

There is no yardstick to tell you how much is too much time to spend with your deaf child. Some people would say that it can never be too much. Certainly, you can never spend too much time talking and listening to what your deaf child has to say. But if you are uncertain about the time factor, you may want to complete the following chart that will provide you with a snapshot of a week in your life at home:

Day	Activity	Time Spent Doing Activity	Did Your Child Participate? Yes/No
Monday			
Tuesday			
Wednesday			
Thursday			
Friday			
Saturday			
Sunday			

Creating Literacy Experiences in the Home

There are several things that can be done around the home that can help prepare your deaf child for reading and writing or give him practice in reading and writing activities. While your child's age and language level will very much influence some of these, others will be suitable for children with a wide range of abilities. Below are some suggestions for setting up your home so that it invites your deaf child to engage in literacy experiences.

Labels

These are especially good for young children, a point that was made by one Deaf adult describing her early introduction to reading and writing (see box titled "Labels 'R Us"). Label as many things in your

---

Labels 'R Us

Placing labels on items in the house might seem like a trite activity to some people. After all, the names of many of these items are so common. This might be true for a hearing child who has a strong command of English. We cannot, however, make the same assumption for deaf children. Think about how many times you have used the words *sink, spatula, can opener, DVD player, dining room hutch, closet, drawer, couch,* and other words with your deaf child. Frances realized that she was not using many household words with her seven-year-old deaf daughter Deanna. With a pen and masking tape in hand, she decided to label as many things as she could in her house. She then had Deanna read the words and memorize how to spell them. Deanna did this by repeatedly fingerspelling the names. To add a little excitement to this, Frances would occasionally give a pop quiz. Frances would walk to an object, cover the label with her hand, and ask Deanna to spell the word. She would also spell out an item and Deanna would have to locate it. Deanna came to look forward to the challenge of acing her mom's quizzes.

---

house as you can. If your child uses sign language, you may wish to include pictures of signs along with some of the labels. Or you could have a sign for a particular item in some places and a word in other places. For example, some chairs can have the word *chair* on them, whereas others can have a picture of the sign for CHAIR. Do not simplify this task by using easy words. If a chair is better referred to as a barstool then call it this. The wider variety of words you use, the better in the long run, but you may wish to stick with just the more common names at the beginning of this activity. At a later stage, you can expand the vocabulary by using other terms for the same or similar objects.

Couch: sofa, love seat, davenport, divan, futon

Chair: armchair, seat, chaise, LaZ-Boy, recliner, lounger, wing chair

Rug: carpet, floor mat, throw rug, broadloom, runner

Paper: notepad, tablet, notebook, foolscap, pad

Notes

Leave notes for your child. Begin this when they are just starting to read and continue until they are advanced readers. A note for a beginning reader might simply say

Robert,

Brush your teeth. Go to bed.

Love, Dad.

While a note for a thirteen-year-old might read,

Rachel,

I had to leave because our friend Jeremy Olmstead managed to snatch two tickets for tomorrow's football game. He's leaving on a business trip tonight, so I had to go over to pick up the tickets. There's shepherd's pie in the fridge. Please pre-heat the oven to 350 degrees then pop the pie in for forty-five minutes. I'll be home at 5:30.

Love, Mom.

Communicate by TTY

When the TTY began making its way into the homes of deaf people in the 1970s, it was a landmark in the facilitation of independence for the Deaf community. It also highlighted the importance of literacy skills as a mainstay in the lives of deaf people. Parents of young deaf children should introduce their child to the use of a TTY through modeling. They can have their deaf child stand beside them while carrying on a typed conversation with someone else on the TTY. In this way, the deaf child soon learns that a TTY is yet another way of communicating with someone and that there is a specific convention for using it appropriately. They learn, for example, that GA (go ahead) is the symbol for turn-taking, that it is important not to type too long before letting the other person contribute to the conversation, the way to sign off, and other nuances about TTY procedures and protocol. In time, they will be able to use it in a like manner and for similar purposes as their same-age hearing peers use the phone. Neeley (2000) tells how her deaf daughter Rebecca began to type on a TTY with her deaf friend Lindsay.

> In kindergarten, as Lindsay and Becca's emerging literacy skills continued to develop, they began to type and read familiar words during TTY conversations. At first they typed their names at the beginning of the conversation. Then they learned to type "here." This was an easy word because the "e" and "r" are adjacent on the keyboard. They also learned to hit the spacebar between words. Soon Becca could independently dial Lindsay's house and upon seeing an answer type, "Becca here GA." (24)

Not everyone has a TTY, and it will likely be the case that many of your deaf child's hearing friends and acquaintances will not have one. You can, however, tell these people to dial 711, the nationwide number for using a message relay center (MRC). Anyone dialing this number will be connected to an operator who can connect the caller with a TTY user. The operator types the messages that the caller is saying and reads aloud the messages that the person on the TTY is typing. Allowing his friends and relatives to talk directly to your deaf child over a phone line exposes him to more opportunities to engage in authentic and unmediated conversations.

Communicate by E-mail

Take advantage of this new media in today's electronic culture. After all, everyone else does. E-mail and on-line conversations have been a boon to deaf people of all ages. And every child loves to open up the computer and find messages waiting for him in the inbox. Because you know your child so well, you can readily send messages that are understandable and of interest to him. Your child, in turn, will be able to send you messages when you are at work, when he is at school, or when he is in the mood to send an e-mail message rather than saying something to you. An important point about e-mail is that the message itself is authentic because it is sent at a time when the child really wants to say something. There is also an additional spin-off in that it provides you with a perfect opportunity to introduce new vocabulary and to use sentence structures that are challenging to your deaf child.

Display Books and Magazines

In addition to taking your child to the library, you should have a library or bookshelves in your home with books and magazines on them—not just videos. Stock your home library with books and magazines that you enjoy reading as well as with those that appeal to your deaf child. Young children love to read books over and over again so do not feel compelled to buy lots of books, because the public library always has plenty of reading material for people of all ages. However, it is not difficult to have some books on hand for reading. Bazaars, garage sales, thrift stores, and annual sell-offs at libraries are excellent sources for cheap high-quality books. Picture magazines such as *National Geographic* are good to have on hand and can often be bought for as little as a dime each at second-hand bookshops. Many schools have flyers distributed by publishing companies that sell books at greatly discounted prices. Keep in mind that one of the purposes of the home library is to demonstrate to your child that you value reading. Even if he does not spend much time reading, at the very least, you can give him the opportunity to do so in his own home.

Start a Dialogue Journal

Dialogue journals are used by teachers as a way of stimulating their students to write. In schools, they are simply a written dialogue between the teacher and the child. What the child writes about is secondary to the fact that he is writing about something to someone who is important and who enjoys reading his message. It could be about something the child did, likes, wants to do, feels, or anything else he wants to share. The teacher then reads the dialogue and writes a response. Parents, too, can use the dialogue journal as a way of stimulating their deaf child to write. Some parents encourage their children to write one paragraph everyday after school to say what they had done that day. Typically, dialogue journals are not this restrictive, and the choice of topics is usually open to whatever it is that the child wants to write about. Moreover, this is not the time for the parents to make corrections in grammar, although there may be the odd occasion when you can use your child's enthusiasm to gently introduce a new word that helps capture what he is trying to say, as in the following example.

In the child's journal entry:

In morning, I go see Monica. Monica forgot tie up her dog. I run away before the dog bited me.

Father's response in journal:

I am so pleased that you <u>escaped</u> before the dog <u>bit</u> you.

Notice how, in one short sentence, the father introduces the word *escape* and gives the correct form for the past tense of the irregular verb *bite*. After the child has read the response, the father can then find a time to explain what the words *escape* and *bit* mean without making a big deal of it.

Why Playing Is Good for You and Your Deaf Child

Play is an important and oftentimes forgotten activity in the intellectual, emotional, social, and linguistic development of a child. If you play with your child, you are likely going to communicate with your child a lot more. Even if this talk is nonsense, it is still important to the child who is using his conversation with a parent to create a make-believe world.

Child: You go to bed now. [Points under a blanket held up by four chairs.]

Mother: But I am not tired. I want to watch TV.

Child: No. You go to sleep now. You got to go to doctor when you wake up.

Mother: Okay. Where's my Piggy? [Looks around the room for her child's favorite stuffed animal.]

Child: [Can't find Piggy so she gives mother a Lego piece.] This is Piggy. Now sleep.

Mother: [Thirty seconds later.] That was a good nap. I'm hungry now. I want to eat.

Child: [Puts plastic food on a plate and pretends to pour milk in a cup.] Eat this. Don't make a mess.

In all play situations, cooperation between the participants is essential, and talking is important for ensuring that the participants understand each other. Debra Lively, an early childhood expert who has had extensive experience with deaf preschoolers and their parents, noted that play is an excellent activity for facilitating parent–child interactions that are nonthreatening and free of many of the day-to-day frustrations experienced by children. In her interactions with parents, Lively emphasized the importance of talking as a way of managing play time and giving the deaf child an opportunity to play with language too. From her perspective, "words take the place of reality." Another major benefit is that parents are able to influence the play situation in such a way that the child is encouraged to use high-order thinking skills, such as the abilities to

- Solve problems
- Reason through symbolic play
- Puzzle out logical operations
- Test hypotheses
- Be creative
- Experiment with language
- Develop social skills

We concur with this assessment. We also want to stress the social importance of your child playing with others and especially with same-age peers in a variety of spontaneous, unstructured play situations.

The Great Shopping Trip

The shopping trip can be every parent's elixir for stimulating vocabulary growth in their deaf child and exposing him to the printed word. For preschoolers and beginning readers, shopping provides a great opportunity for introducing concepts, such as the ones listed below and the examples that follow them.

- Names of food and other shopping list items: cereal, corn on the cob, backpack, shirts, jumpsuits, sandals, etc.
- Types of stores: grocery store, clothing store, hardware store, deli, bookstore, etc.
- Routines: "After shopping, we have to stop and get gas for the car"; "We'll use the ATM to get some money and then go shopping"; "We will shop first, go to the park, and then go home."
- General observations: "There are not many people shopping today;" "It's raining. We will try to park close to the shoe store;" "The car feels so hot because we left it sitting in the hot sun for two hours."

For more advanced readers, shopping presents a greater variety of opportunities for reading.

- Large print: Red-tag Sale, Annual Winter Blowout Sale, 1/2 Off Everything in Store, Mother's Day Special, X-mas Savings, etc.
- Labels: low-fat and low-cal foods, 1% partly skimmed milk, whole wheat and multigrain bread, 50% cotton/polyester T-shirt, wrinkle-free pants, apple juice from concentrate, unsweetened, etc.
- Informational: Receipts needed to return merchandise, R & J's Shoes closed for renovations. Re-opening 6/17, One free taco if Thunderbirds win by 5 or more runs. Must bring ticket stub.

Shopping is important, but simply walking through stores is not enough for linguistic and intellectual growth. Parents and their deaf child should engage in meaningful conversation. What's meaningful? The three case examples presented earlier in this chapter showed conversations that were devoid of any real sense of intellectual involvement on the part of the child. The parental expectation was for the child to merely say something simple. Meaningful conversations, on the other hand, are linked to topics of interest to the child, with a very liberal use of the word *interest.* Situations that can lead to meaningful conversations include the following:

1. Asking for a child's opinion

   - What kind of purse should Mommy buy?
   - We are having roast chicken for dinner. What kind of vegetable will be good to eat with chicken?
   - We have to buy something for your older sister's birthday. What are some things that you think she might like?

2. Describing something that the child has just seen

   - Did you see that flash of light? What do you think it was? What kinds of things make a big flash of light?
   - Those people who just walked passed us are our neighbors. Why do you think they are in this garden store?

3. Asking the child to explain why they want something

   - For the past three weeks, you have been asking me to buy you a new volleyball. If I buy you a new ball, when will you play with it? Who will play with you?

- You want a new long-sleeve shirt? You have lots of shirts at home. Why do you need another one?
- I have not been in that store before. It looks interesting. You came here two days ago with your father. What's inside?

4. Talking in general terms

- I like it when you come shopping with me. You help me to remember some of the things that I need to buy. What do you like best about shopping?
- Why do you think malls have so many stores? How come this mall is always busy on Friday nights?
- It's raining heavy outside. Let's stay inside the mall until the rain lightens up and then go to our car. Are there any stores that you would like to visit now? Why would you like to go to that store?

An Example from the Classroom

John Miller teaches deaf children in St. Louis, a small rural town in the middle of Michigan. He has taught at the preschool and kindergarten levels for eleven years, and during his first few years, he was constantly bewildered with the low vocabulary levels of his students at the beginning of the school year. One of his biggest challenges as a teacher was getting parents to spend more time doing things with their deaf children and talking to them. Just telling this to the parents did not meet with much success, therefore, he got permission from his supervisor to conduct a semester-long experiment that would include the option of parents joining the class on a weekly shopping trip to the grocery store.

Before he began the experiment, he tested his preschoolers on eighty vocabulary words relating to food and eating. These were common words that he felt all preschoolers should know and included names of food (e.g., *carrot, bread, milk, peach, butter*) and other words related to shopping and eating (e.g., *buy, store, chewing*). Six children took the test at the beginning of the experiment, and the highest score was 14 out of 80. At the end of the four-month experiment, every child scored 100 percent on the same test. Here's how he did it.

1. The class went on a weekly field trip to a local grocery store, and parents, grandparents, or significant others in the deaf children's lives were invited to join.
2. Each child was given a list of two things that they had to buy at the store. At school, they were shown the sign or fingerspelling of the word, and some of the children were also shown how to pronounce the word. A picture of the sign for the word was pasted in a booklet and given to the children and their parents.
3. At the store, each child had his own small shopping basket and had to look for the item on their list. The family members and teachers who accompanied the child were encouraged to talk, saying things such as

   • Where can we find the butter?
   • Should we go to the left or to the right?
   • Yum. That cake looks good. Look at the pretty colors on it.
   • This is a big shopping cart. I will push it, but you have to tell me where to go.

4. The child was given cash to pay for the items, and then the class returned to the school.
5. In the classroom, the teacher reviewed the items that were bought, showing the students the printed word, a picture of the sign, the signs and/or fingerspelling, and saying the spoken word. The class talked about the trip, and the food was put away for a cooking activity that would take place later. During the cooking activity, the teacher again reviewed the words that were studied on the field trip.

Early in the experiment, the adults had to provide much guidance. But each week, the children gained in experience and confidence so much that, by the end of the experiment, they were able to read the words on the shopping list and locate the item in the store—which they did with much enthusiasm. Since the initial experiment, John Miller has made this activity a mainstay in his classroom.

Getting Started with a List of Things to Do

Leonardo da Vinci kept a to-do list much like millions of other people around the world. A to-do list is simply a list of things that you are planning to do today or at some point in the future. The beauty of this type of list is that you are in control of shaping future experiences. Writing the list is also a good intellectual activity because you think through the things that you have to do and want to do. It forces you to consider your priorities. Every to-do list is personal, and whereas some may be fanciful.

- Retire at age thirty.
- Build a log mansion in the mountains of Montana.
- Date a movie star.

Most are practical.

- Get the lawn mower fixed.
- Water the garden.
- Take Michael to his bowling game at 4:00.
- Write a note to Judith's teacher about the homework assignment.

Another way of looking at a to-do list is to think of it as being a list of experiences yet to come. Leonardo da Vinci, the genius who painted the *Mona Lisa* and *The Last Supper*, wrote the following to-do list during the Renaissance.

Show how clouds form and dissolve,

How water vapor rises from the earth to the air,

How mists form and air thickens,

And why one wave seems more blue than another;

Describe the aerial regions,

And the causes of snow and hail,

How water condenses, and hardens into ice,

And how new figures form in the air,

And new leaves on the trees,

And icicles on the stones of cold places. . . . (Gelb 1998, 222)

With this list, Leonardo was shaping his future. He was purposefully planning to place himself in a position where new ideas would flow forth and where he would be forced to find new words and sentences to capture his thoughts.

You too, are in the position to shape the future by planning to do things with your deaf child. In this way, you will place your child in a situation where new words can be learned and put into sentences that capture his thoughts about his experiences. The ten examples below for an older deaf child should help you get started with your own to-do list. Note how short each activity on the list is.

1. Observe the sky on a clear night. Some words to talk about are *Venus, dusk (sundown), horizon, star, planet.*

   Make the following points:

   - Venus is the first star in the evening sky. It always appears on the western horizon at dusk.
   - Venus is a planet like Earth.
   - Venus is not a star because it doesn't give off its own light.
   - Venus is between the Earth and the sun.
   - The sun is shining on Venus. That's why we can see it at night when the sky is dark.
   - Dusk is that time of the evening when the sun disappears beyond the horizon.

   Follow up with pictures of Venus and Earth from a book about planets.

2. Take a different route to the store. Some words to talk about are *direction, neighborhood, different, alternative, route.*

   Make the following points:

   - What's different about this way to the store?
   - The way you go someplace is called the route.

- What are some different directions that can be taken to the store?
- When might this route be a good alternative route for going to the store?

3. Eat out at a Thai (or some other ethnic) restaurant. Some words to talk about are: *Thailand, Thai, ethnic, spicy, menu, Asia, foreign.*

   Make the following points:

   - When we talk about things relating to the country of Thailand, we use the word *Thai*. This is the same as using the word *American* to talk about things relating to the United States or using the word *Canadian* to talk about things relating to Canada.
   - Thailand is a country in Southeast Asia.
   - This restaurant is an ethnic restaurant.
   - The Thai language is a foreign language.
   - The menu has foreign names on it that most adults do not understand.
   - Thai food can be very spicy.

4. Go to the playground in a park. Some words to talk about are *slide, swings, bars, bridge, ladder.*

   Make the following points:

   - What are the different ways to make a swing move (pushing; moving your legs up and down)?
   - Which slide is the longest? The fastest? The most fun?
   - How many bars can you cross before falling?
   - What are the different ways to make the bridge wiggle?
   - How many different types of ladders are there in the whole playground? How can they be described?

5. Go to a baseball game. Some words to talk about are *innings, strikes, balls, umpire, vendors, home plate, concession stand, fly ball, bunt, home run, catcher, first base.*

   Make the following points:

   - Describe the rules of the game.
   - Explain what the home plate umpire and other umpires do.

- Explain what the various signals mean.
- Describe what a vendor does (i.e., sells peanuts, soda pop, and cotton candy while walking through the stands).
- Describe what a concession stand is.
- Read the number of balls and hits from the scoreboard.

6. Go for a bike ride. Some words to talk about are *exercise, helmet, safety, alert, bicycle/bike riding, tire.*

   Make the following points:

   - The words *bike* and *bicycle* mean the same thing.
   - Bike riding is fun and a good way to exercise.
   - Why should people wear helmets when riding a bike?
   - Why do people need to practice safety when cycling?
   - How do cyclists indicate the direction they will travel to cars and other cyclists?
   - Why do bike riders need to be alert at all times when riding?

7. Pick strawberries (or any other type of fruit that grows in your area). Some words to talk about are *jam, jelly, u-pick, ready-pick, cheaper, country, satisfying.*

   Make the following points:

   - How are u-pick strawberries different than ready-pick strawberries?
   - Why do you think u-pick strawberries are cheaper?
   - Why are strawberry farms in the country and not in the city?
   - How many strawberries are needed to make one pound of jam?
   - Why is doing something for oneself is satisfying?

8. Get a haircut. Some words to talk about are *haircut, hairstyle, barber, clippers, walk-ins, appointment.*

   Make the following points:

   - How often do we get haircuts?
   - Why do people have different hairstyles?
   - What is a barber? What is a hairstylist?

- How long does it take to get a haircut?
- Why do some places require appointments, whereas others allow walk-ins?

9. Go to an automatic car wash. Some words to talk about are *automatic, touch-free, rinse, wax, cycle.*

   Make the following points:

   - Why is something called automatic? What does an automatic car wash do?
   - What is a touch-free car wash? What are other methods of washing a car?
   - What does the rinse cycle do? What would happen if the car was not rinsed?
   - What does the wax cycle do? What happens to the car paint if it is not waxed?
   - How long does it take from the time the car enters the car wash to the time it exits?

10. Clean the garage (basement, closet, pantry, etc.). Some words to talk about are *garage, junk, tools, recycling, garbage.*

    Make the following points:

    - Why do we need to clean out the garage every now and again?
    - What things in the garage can be called junk? What do we do with junk?
    - What type of tools are found in a garage (e.g., gardening, carpentry)?
    - What things in the garage can be recycled?
    - What can be done to stop the garage from filling up with garbage?

You can increase the learning experience associated with each of the above activities by writing out the vocabulary and the questions on index cards. This would make it easier to repeat the activity at a later time. Young children, especially, love routines, and all children like to show what they have learned. Recalling an experience will help a child remember words that he has recently learned.

It does not take much time to write out a single to-do list. Moreover, if you only compiled one a week, that would be fifty-two lists in a year. That's fifty-two authentic learning experiences enhanced with meaningful conversations. Doing this will make you the Leonardo da Vinci of your household.

Conclusion

For your deaf child to have a reason to communicate, he must know something about the world in which he lives; and this knowledge is gained through experiences that can be readily organized by the parents. We are *not* proposing drills or naming tasks or other similar exercises to elicit language but rather suggesting activities that are natural interactions (i.e., have a social context). We therefore encourage real conversation and spontaneous communication during all kinds of everyday activities and in play.

The knowledge a child gains through authentic world experiences motivates him to name objects and agents and to explore the relationship between them. As Nelson (1966) points out, although cognition may be an antecedent to language, language plays an important role in mediating cognitive development. In other words, thinking and language are inextricably interwoven, with each one supporting the other. This chapter on experience suggests that the major task for parents, and it is not a very difficult one, is to ensure that they do all they can to enlarge the social and experiential life of their deaf child rather than restrict it. The skills the child will develop from these authentic conversations and social activities, including play, will certainly enhance his contextual learning of language. So, it all really does begin with experience.

CHAPTER 6

Literacy in the World of TV

This chapter will help you understand

- The challenges that deaf children face when reading captions
- What you can do to help your deaf child recognize and understand symbols and print that are used to explain sound-related events on TV
- A variety of ways in which you can help your deaf child adjust to the reading of captions on TV
- A set of principles that can be used to help your deaf child learn to read and understand captions on TV

One day after school, four deaf children, two sets of brothers and sisters aged seven, eleven, twelve, and thirteen, were at home watching a program on a thirty-inch TV. They all had college-educated Deaf parents who expected these children to go on to college because they were doing very well in the school they all attended. One of the authors of this book was sitting among them and was also watching the program. After a few minutes, it dawned on him that the program was not captioned. Also, the cartoon made absolutely no sense whatsoever. The characters on the screen were racing here and there, chasing each other from one place to another, and fighting furiously. The plot? Anyone's guess.

So he nudged the girl named Joni who was sitting next to him and asked, "What's happening? Why don't you watch a program that is captioned?"

"This show is captioned," she said quickly and then turned her attention back to the screen.

"Then why don't you turn the captioning on?" he asked.

"Because it interferes with the action in the picture," Joni answered.

In the early 1980s, when just a handful of TV programs were closed-captioned, viewers had to have a special decoding device that would allow the captions to appear on the screen. Not every deaf person owned one, but for those who did, these decoders were treasured and were quite the status symbol within the Deaf community.

Since its inception, captioning on television has been heralded as one of the greatest technologies ever to affect the lives of deaf people. It made TV accessible and meaningful to the deaf population and expanded their viewing habits. In the early days of TV, action thrillers enthralled deaf people because, although they might not be able to understand the dialogue, they could still enjoy the action sequences. With the advent of captioning, however, they could now enjoy a variety of programming. And as they did, it dawned on many of them that captioning was also a tremendous help in expanding their own English vocabulary.

Today, all programs on major TV networks are captioned during evening prime time. Captioning covers sitcoms, children's shows, movies, news, presidential addresses, cartoons, and sports. Adult content TV programs and even infomercials are being captioned. In fact, some stations are close to offering twenty-four hours of captioning everyday. An increasing number of commercials are also captioned.

Echoing the sentiments of deaf adults, parents also claim that captioning gives their deaf children more opportunities to improve their reading skills.

> Many parents will confirm the benefits that reading captions has on the reading skills of their deaf children . . . and the value is not all related to reading and English skills. Television is a cultural icon and as such is a significant provider of information about one's own society and that of others. (Stewart and Kluwin 2001, 323)

So why did a bright girl like Joni in the story above turn off the captions? Was it really because the printed words on the TV screen interfered with the picture? This is a question that you are going to have to ask yourself when your deaf child is watching a program that is captioned. In this chapter, we are going to take you through a number of activities that will help you understand some of the challenges that deaf people face when watching a captioned program.

Initiating the Parent into the World of Captioning

Hearing parents readily understand the value of captioning to an audience who cannot hear a soundtrack and, therefore, are unable to make sense of TV dialogue. Similarly, it seems obvious that once captions are provided on the screen, deaf people will have access to information that is needed to fully enjoy a program. As far as the theory goes, both of these statements are accurate, but they come with a caveat. Understanding the value of captioning does not, by itself, guarantee that parents will know how to ensure that their deaf child will get the most benefit from watching captions.

Two analogies may help clarify the position. The first stems from parents who use American Sign Language (ASL) or some form of signed communication with their deaf child. It is critical for a deaf child, who relies on the use of signing as his primary means of communication, that he receives much exposure to signing. For parents, this could mean that they always sign in the presence of their deaf child, that they practice to gain some degree of fluency in their signing ability, and that they use signs for meaningful communication. Thus, it is not solely a parent's ability to sign that is the key to this deaf child's acquisition of language and knowledge but also the manner in which parents use their signing skills.

The second analogy relates to those parents who have a deaf child who wears hearing aids or has a cochlear implant. Neither of these devices, by themselves, leads to proficient speech and hearing skills. For those children who do attain some degree of benefit, it is very likely that they have parents who are committed to helping them use these listening devices. Help from parents comes in a great variety of ways, including ensuring that the batteries are good and that the devices are functioning properly, prompting the child to speak clearly, expecting the deaf child to make every effort to listen carefully, and providing positive feedback for his attempts to speak and listen. In other words, behind every successful hearing aid or cochlear implant user are strongly supportive parents or significant others in the deaf child's life.

The lesson we can learn from these examples of using sign language or listening devices is that merely turning captioning on is not enough. The following two activities should convince you of the significance of this statement. These activities were first described in Stewart and Kluwin (2001) and are further elaborated upon here.

Step One: Turn Off the Sound and the Captions

Everyone has, at one time or another, watched TV for a short period without the sound or captions on. This can occur in a department store where forty televisions are showing the same program, in a bar or restaurant where there are TV sets all around the walls, or at a friend's place where the sound is turned off to herald your arrival. What have you learned from these incidental experiences, especially when the program that is on is not sports related? Probably nothing that you did not already know: When the sound is off, you can't follow the dialogue. Moreover, if you were not interested in the program that was being shown, you really did not care about what was being said. But what if you really did care and wanted to know what was going on?

Select at least four TV programs, other than sports, that you normally watch along with one or two children's programs that your deaf child watches. Include in your selection a variety of programming, such as a report from your local station's evening news, a sitcom, a PBS or Discovery channel documentary, a talk show, a Saturday morning cartoon, and a PBS educational program for children. Create a chart as shown in figure 6.1, write down the names of these programs, and then set aside a time to watch them. You might be wondering what the point of this activity is when you already know that you will not be able to understand most, if not all, the dialogue in each program. This activity, in fact, has two major goals.

Name of TV Program	Ease of Speech-reading	Use of Facial Cues	Nature of Other Visual Cues	Strategies for Under-standing	Overall Comprehension & Enjoyment

Adapted with permission from D. Stewart and T. Kluwin. 2001. *Teaching Deaf and Hard of Hearing Students: Content, Strategies, and Curriculum.* Boston: Allyn & Bacon.

Figure 6.1. Experience chart for watching TV without captions and sound

1. To alert you to the emotions that you experience as you stare at a soundless or, more generally, a virtually language-less TV screen for an extended period of time
2. To alert you to the cognitive tools that you use as you seek alternative means to gain information about what is being said

When you do this activity, watch the entire program that you have selected. Do not cut it short thinking that you have already gained the experience that you need. Deaf children do not always have the option of walking away from a program that they do not understand as, for example, when they are watching an uncaptioned film at a movie theater. A deaf child may also be under social pressure to watch an uncaptioned TV program simply because other people want to watch it. Therefore, by watching the entire program, you will be more likely to develop a greater empathy for some of his experiences.

As you complete the chart for each program, you will likely find yourself becoming increasingly frustrated with this activity and aching to simply turn on the sound or, at the very least, the captions. If you persisted in watching each program to the end, you might also have discovered that you focused on clues for understanding that you had either never noticed before or had always taken for granted. In addition, you may have become quite anxious and restless as you struggled to understand what was going on.

Compare your completed chart with the following sample of observations that we made.

Ease of Speechreading

Speechreading someone on TV is very difficult and, in fact, it is all but impossible to read the lips of many actors. Contextual clues play a major role when one is unable to speechread parts of the dialogue. For example, if on the game show *Who Wants To Be a Millionaire?* the contestant says "B. Plutonium. Final answer," you will likely understand what was said because of the number of contextual clues. You were able to read the list of possible answers beforehand; the letter *B* is distinguishable from *A, C,* and *D;* you might have known that the correct answer was "B" and therefore anticipated that response; and the contestant might have made obvious facial expressions and body movements that signaled that she or he was ready to answer the question.

Use of Facial Cues

You might find yourself focusing more on the actors' faces than on the picture as a whole. The emotions of actors are largely conveyed through their facial expressions, thus, we can often tell if someone is angry, delighted, suspicious, clueless, and so forth just by their appearance. Are they also speaking rapidly? Then perhaps that is a sign of anger or high anxiety but certainly not one of melancholy or a sorrowful confession. Are the eyes shifting? If so, this might indicate that the actor is glancing in the direction of noise, is gazing at other people not visible on the screen, or is expecting something to happen.

Nature of Other Visual Cues

A wavy picture usually indicates that an actor is lapsing into a dream or is recalling an event. A black-and-white scene often relates to the past, and slow motion foretells many events, including a dramatic change in the scenario, such as an explosion, death, or peacefulness. Print on the screen is an invaluable source of information and gives a wide variety of clues about the picture, ranging from the location and year of a scene to the theme of a talk show program. Maps and diagrams also sometimes provide useful information about the dialogue.

Strategies for Understanding

What did you do to help you understand a program better? Many strategies work, but quite possibly the single most important factor was your own knowledge and experience relating to what you were watching. For example, an evening news report about a submarine sinking in the Arctic Ocean will be more understandable if you have already read about it in the newspaper or on a news Web site. A documentary about baseball will make more sense to a baseball fan. Watching a rerun is typically easier to follow. Some programs, such as *Sesame Street*, are more predictable than others, and parts of them may not require much dialogue to help a viewer's comprehension. You might have found yourself creating and recreating your own plot for a particular show on the basis of what you were able to gather from the visuals. Was your plot correct? Perhaps not, but the activity is intellectually stimulating and heightens your senses for additional clues to help you construct a plot as well as to check it for accuracy as the program proceeds.

Now think about which of the above strategies you used plus others that would be good for helping your deaf child enjoy a TV program and then compare them with a list of suggestions that we provide later in this chapter, beginning on page 130.

Step Two: Turn Off the Sound and Turn on the Captions

The above activity is repeated, but this time the captions are turned on and you use the chart shown in figure 6.2. You may select differ-

Name of TV Program	Speed of Captions	Accuracy of Captions (spelling, etc.)	Visual Cues Presented by Captions	Complexity of Language and Vocabulary	Strategies for Reading Captions

Adapted with permission from D. Stewart and T. Kluwin. 2001. *Teaching Deaf and Hard of Hearing Students: Content, Strategies, and Curriculum.* Boston: Allyn & Bacon.

Figure 6.2. Experience chart for watching TV with captions but without sound

ent programs or the same programs that you had selected in the first step. The goals of this activity are:

1. To develop an awareness of the challenges that reading captioning on TV presents to deaf children
2. To explore strategies that can help a person understand captions and enjoy a TV program more

Doing the tasks described in this activity will better prepare parents to help deaf children use whatever reading capacities they have to watch and enjoy a captioned program.

For some or all of the programs that you watch, you should tape the program first. This will allow you to make notes and not miss out on what is being said on TV. You will also be able to rewind parts and review sections that, for various reasons, you might have missed. (This is the key reason why many deaf adults prefer an evening of rented videos than standard TV fare. If they are visually distracted from a program, or if they miss what was printed in the captions, or if they were so absorbed by the captions that they missed out seeing the picture, then it becomes convenient to hit the rewind button on the remote control.) Finally, you should watch the programs again with *both* the sound and captioning on to see if the captions match the dialogue.

With the captions turned on, one difference that you will notice immediately is that you understand what the program is about and that your enjoyment level is much higher than it was when you had the captions and the sound switched off. You were probably more relaxed as you watched the captions and certainly not as stressed out by the anxiety caused by not knowing what was happening on the tube. And yet for many of you, your foray into watching a program with no sound and just captions will catch you off-guard. Did you notice the occasional misspelling, instances when the captions would suddenly disappear, the seemingly high-speed scrolling of the captions, and other problems? If so, then you have made a good first step toward understanding communication from a caption reader's perspective.

With your chart completed, compare what you have written with the examples listed below.

Speed of Captions

The speed of the captions is highly variable and contingent upon the speed of the dialogue. Programs associated with fast dialogues are quite unpredictable. Evening news programs, talk shows, and sitcoms with highly agitated speakers often have quick-paced dialogues and fast captions, as do some cartoon shows and programs for young children where characters talk back and forth to one another very rapidly. If you felt yourself reaching for the volume control but resisting the temptation, chalk that up to a maturing appreciation for the complexity of TV literacy for deaf children.

Accuracy of Captions

Several types of common inaccuracies that occur with captions are misspelled words, captions appearing before the dialogue is spoken, a significant lag between when the dialogue was spoken and the captions appeared, and an absence of captions for some of the dialogue.

Visual Cues Presented by Captions

Good captioning alerts the viewers to all of the sounds in a program. If music is playing, then you might see the words [Classical music playing] or [Music playing] or simply musical notes. Sounds from actions occurring off screen are noted as [Gunshots], [Baby crying], [Soft sobbing], [Humming], [Tires squealing], [Thunder], or whatever else describes the sounds being made.

Complexity of Language and Vocabulary

No matter how well you can read, there will be a caption somewhere that will make you hesitate and want to reread it. Perhaps, the sentence was awkward or perhaps it simply made no sense, which sometimes happens when a person being interviewed utters an unfinished sentence. Many children's programs use short sentences, but these short sentences may contain colloquial vocabulary, jargon, or nonsensical words that rhyme with other words. Or the dialogue may move quickly from one person to another with words and modifications of idioms, such as in the following transcript taken from the popular Canadian educational program "The Magic School Bus: In the Rainforest." This program is aimed at elementary and middle school children.

Speaker: You are now leaving the mud-free zone. Beware of the peccaries, the bugs, and the filthy mud.

Student #1:   Man, Inspector #47 has got a thing about mud.

Student #2:   And I've a hunch it has something to do with the missing cacao beans.

Miss Frizzle: A connection worth detection, Tim?

Student #1:   But Miss Frizzle, what could mud possibly have to do with the cacao beans. Besides we're searching for teeny insects.

Student #3:   Is it just me or are we about to get down and muddy with a pack of peccaries?!

Strategies for Reading Captions

A common complaint about captions is that a viewer can miss the picture while reading the captions, especially when there is little break in the dialogue. Does it then make sense to always take in the picture first and then read the captions? If you focus on the captioning, how can you obtain clues from the actor's face? Or do you still need these clues when captioning is available? The strategies that you as a hearing parent use are likely to be idiosyncratic. You must also remember that you bring a firm grasp of English, an extensive vocabulary, and a great many personal experiences to the situation. However, there are strategies that you can use to help deaf children who have yet to master reading or who do not have an extensive vocabulary, and these are discussed below.

Helping Deaf Children Develop Skills for Reading Captions

Stewart and Kluwin (2001) identified the following six ways in which parents can help their deaf children meet the challenge of reading captions:

1. Have the captions turned on at all times. Show that captioning is a part of the family's TV culture and not just something that is turned on in the presence of deaf children. Leaving the captioning on, whenever the TV is turned on, demonstrates to a deaf child that his communication need is a valued part of how the family functions.
2. Watch TV and videos with your deaf child. Find out which programs are your child's favorite and take the time to watch some of them. If the timing of the programs does not allow you to watch them with him then you might wish to tape them and watch them later. Taping a program also gives you the opportunity to watch the program more than once, to stop it at anytime to talk about what is happening, and to review words and sentences.
3. Explain to your deaf child what is happening in a show. This will make it easier for the child to understand the captions and will certainly make it easier for him to follow the plot.

4. Explain the meaning of visual cues that appear as a part of the captioning. These cues come in a variety of forms such as musical notes to indicate music, or text in brackets to describe action that can be heard occurring elsewhere such as a dog barking or a siren blaring.

5. If the captions help you understand what is being said on TV then tell this to your deaf child. Provide real examples, such as it helped you learn the spelling of a name or a word or it helped you understand what was being said because you could not understand what the speaker was saying.

6. Use captioned programs as a means of communicating with your deaf child. Captioned TV by itself is not an adequate substitute for direct communication but the time you spend with your child discussing a program provides an excellent language learning opportunity. (326)

The overall message that these suggestions carry is that captioning must be valued, it must be shown to be beneficial to everyone in the family, and parents must spend time helping their deaf child understand the techniques that will facilitate their enjoyment of a program. To these suggestions we add the following key points, which can guide a parent's interaction with a deaf child in front of the TV.

Familiarity

Familiarity provides a strong foundation upon which to build reading skills. Familiarity is a rock in the lives of young children. Seeing familiar faces and having the same routines, hearing the same voices, or seeing the same signing all lead to reassurance and enable a child to learn better. Familiarity is also the key to effective communication because it makes speechreading or understanding a person's signing easier. Draw upon the power of familiarity by establishing routines for watching TV programs that appeal to your child. Select a few programs that he can watch at a regular time and include programs that you will watch with him. Make it a habit to routinely talk about the program during commercial breaks and/or after the show is over. There is always something that can be said and questions that can be asked. Draw upon the routines presented in the shows to formulate some of the things that you might say to your child.

Repetition

Watch an episode of a program over and over again. Just as children like to hear the same book repeatedly read to them, they also like to watch reruns or a movie again and again. Buy or rent a video that your deaf child likes or tape a favorite TV program, and talk about the show to help your child develop greater familiarity with the characters, themes, and/or routines.

Connect the Caption and the Picture

For the most part, the captions relate directly to the picture that is on the screen. However, there are times when the picture relates to something that was said prior to the picture being shown or after the picture was shown; examples of both are given below.

- Captions precede the picture. On the screen, we see a fashion designer talking about the clothes that teenagers are wearing in high school these days. This is then followed by several camera shots of high school students walking down the hallway or standing around in front of the school.
- Captions follow the picture. We see a film of a basketball player dribbling down the court for a dunk during the last second of a game. We then see that same person sitting in a studio talking about his emotions during those final moments of a game.

While you are watching a program, bring these possibilities of caption and picture arrangements to your deaf child's attention— irrespective of their age—by prompting them and explaining how you figured out what is happening on the screen and its relationship to the captions. An example of how this can be done follows:

Parent: Why do you think there is a film but no captions on
               TV? [The film on TV shows three children playing in a
               park with a mother watching them.]
Deaf child: Because no one is talking.
Parent: Correct. No one is talking. Look. Now there is a
               woman talking, and there are captions. What were the
               captions about?

Deaf child: I am not sure. Talking about a family?

Parent: Yes. She's talking about the difficulties of single parents raising a family. The mother we saw in the film watching her three children playing is a single mother. Now they are talking about that mother and other single parents like her.

Connect the Words and Pictures

A child may know that the animal on TV is a giraffe and that a particular building where people work is called a factory. He may know the spoken word and/or the signs for *giraffe* and *factory.* But he might not know that the sign GIRAFFE is spelled g-i-r-a-f-f-e. The same can be true for a child who knows the meaning of the word *factory* in speech but does not recognize it in print. Therefore, when you see a word in a caption that directly refers to something in the video, take a few seconds to point this out. You may wish to write some of these words down and show them to your child during a commercial break.

Parent: Do you remember seeing the sunset in the film just before the commercial break?

Deaf child: Yes. I know what a sunset is. That is when the sun goes down at nighttime.

Parent: Excellent! Now, look at this word [*dusk* is written on a paper] and tell me what it means.

Deaf child: D-u-s-k looks like the word *dust.* But I don't know what it means.

Parent: Dusk is another word for sunset. It's when the sun disappears on the horizon.

Connect the Words and Signs

ASL does not have a sign for all English words. But it is surprising how often a deaf child will not recognize an English word although he knows the word's sign. This is especially true for signs that can be used for more than one English word. For example, in the list below, the signs in the left column are ones that are typically familiar to many deaf children. But the same signs are used to convey the meaning of the words in the right-hand column, and younger deaf children might not recognize these in print. Make this connection for your deaf child by showing the sign for some of the words that appear in captions.

Common Meaning for a Sign	Other Meanings for the Same Sign
LAND	PROPERTY
OFTEN	FREQUENT
EXCITED	ANXIOUS
MAKE	CREATE
ABOUT	CONCERNING
WAIT	PAUSE
GET	ACQUIRE, OBTAIN, RECEIVE
LATE	TARDY
SICK	ILL

Encourage Deaf Children to Talk about TV and Video Programs

As has been emphasized throughout this book, self-expression (or the act of talking about what one is thinking) is an excellent means for helping a child develop language skills. With thoughtful mediation on the part of a parent, a child's self-expression becomes an opportunity for that child to learn new vocabulary, attach words and sentences to their thoughts, and explore new ways of saying things. Take the following example of a deaf child talking about what he had just read in the captions of a weather report:

Captions: There will be an overnight drop in temperature of 15 degrees that will put temperatures below freezing for the first time this year.

Parent: What does "an overnight drop" means?

Deaf child: Something will be dropped tonight.

Parent: What will be dropped?

Deaf child: The weather will go down.

Parent: Oh, you mean the temperature will go down tonight? Will it happen right now, because it is nighttime already?

Deaf child: It will happen tonight.

Parent: Do you know what *overnight* means? It means throughout the night. So maybe when the sun goes down, it will start to get colder. But by 2:00 a.m., it will be much colder. It doesn't get cold right away. It gets cold over several hours at night. That's what "overnight drop" means.

It is amazing how much language can be expressed and learned from a discussion of just a single sentence. What is even more amazing is that many parents will pass up these opportunities to have meaningful discussions with their deaf child. Yet, the better a child is at expressing himself, the more ready he will be for reading captions that are commensurate with his linguistic abilities.

Encourage Deaf Children to Persevere When Reading Captions

What we do not want deaf children to do is to turn the captions off, because they become frustrated reading them or because they do not even bother to read them. Captioning for deaf children is as important as sound is for hearing children. Hearing children are rarely tempted to turn the sound off on their TV, and it would be even rarer for them to want to watch a whole program without sound. Let your deaf child know that captions are a valued part of a TV program. If the program is not on videotape, then deaf children should not dwell on what it is they might have missed because they could not read nor understand the captions. Explain to them that you too sometimes don't hear or fully understand what was spoken on TV, yet you continue to listen to the program.

Conclusion

It will take patience and perseverance to implement the suggestions that we have made in this chapter. You should begin with the activities that will sensitize you to the challenges that deaf children and deaf adults face when trying to read captions on TV. Following this, you may wish to make just one or two remarks about captioning to your deaf child while watching TV. Some children may be ready and willing to accept interruptions while they are watching TV, but other children may resent any interruptions whatsoever. How you proceed with a plan for helping deaf children read captions is something that you alone can decide. While you are making this decision, bear in mind the following.

1. The role of parents is to enlighten deaf children to the nature of captions and the importance of being able to read them. The better able deaf children are at reading captions, the greater their appreciation of the strength of being a literate viewer.
2. TV is a highly revered icon in our society. Whether you like TV or not and whether you let your children watch a little or a whole lot will depend upon your own value system. Hence, we are not advocating that watching captioned TV is a must for all deaf children. We do, however, believe that reading captions on TV is a special skill—one that does not automatically develop when a child is simply placed in front of a TV set. If you are going to allow your child to watch captioned TV programs then you should take steps to increase his enjoyment and knowledge by being the catalyst in fostering literacy in the world of TV.

CHAPTER 7

Reading

This chapter will help you understand

- Different theories about how children learn to read
- How different approaches to teaching reading can be applied to deaf children
- Reading readiness strategies for young deaf children that can be implemented in the home
- Reading activities for older deaf children

Today, it seems that everyone is concerned about getting children to learn to read. Not only do we aim at becoming a nation of readers with a 100 percent literacy rate, but we want children to begin reading at a young age—younger even than the age at which we began to read. This concern has almost become a national pastime, resulting in an explosion in the number of children's books published over the past twenty years. Many libraries and schools offer reading workshops, and best-selling authors can command million-dollar advances for their books. The magazine shelves at food stores overflow with titles catering to a wide range of interests. Even book catalogs relating to the Deaf community are rapidly adding titles that include picture books, youth fiction, sports, education, and autobiographies. Many parents read to their children nightly, and the Information Age has parents and children alike competing for Internet time on the computer.

Our obsession with reading is a relatively new concern. In the early days of education in the United States, teachers seldom believed that a child could not be taught to read. It would take more than two hundred years of schooling before the terms *remedial reading* and *dyslexia* became popular. Yet, as early as 1655, the French scientist Blaise Pascal reported that by separating syllables into letters and learning the basic sounds, children could be taught to decode written words by sounding them out. Thus, the *phonic* method of teaching reading was born—a method that, at the beginning of the twenty-first century, President George Bush wants installed in U.S. schools.

A second method used first for teaching reading to deaf children stemmed from the work of Thomas Gallaudet and Laurent Clerc (teachers at the first U.S. school for deaf children, founded in 1817). Their method emphasized a controlled vocabulary to help children recognize words by sight rather than by sounding them out. Although this method enjoyed some success in the education of deaf children, an adaptation of it caught on with hearing children and led to the introduction of basal readers in the early 1900s. This series of readers is often referred to as the Dick and Jane books, so named after the books' main characters. With basal readers as one of the cornerstones for beginning readers, there also arrived reading programs that sought to teach reading through a step-by-step process whereby children learned the letters of the alphabet, the forty-four sounds of the English language, and the seventy common ways to spell these sounds. With this foundation, it was believed that children could fluently, accurately, and automatically decode print. Rudolf Flesch (1955) devised this phonic approach and used it to teach his dyslexic grandson to read. This intimate experience with reading instruction led him to write *Why Johnny Can't Read*, which has been lauded by some as one of the greatest educational events of the century.

Toward the end of the twentieth century, the controlled vocabulary of early basal readers and the phonic approach to reading had to move aside as the whole language approach invaded schools under a variety of aliases, including language experience, the psycholinguistic guessing game, whole word, skills in context, and emergent literacy. The proponents of whole language rightly maintain that a love for reading does not arise from drills, worksheets, or stories with decodable texts and a controlled vocabulary. Instead, they want children to be taught to read by being immersed in interesting stories, where words are learned in a context that is enjoyed and understood and where the readers are encouraged to use contextual cues to work out the meaning of a word or a phrase.

However, despite a twenty-year all-out effort in numerous school districts to increase literacy with whole language approaches, the national Right to Read Foundation has come out strongly in favor of returning to the direct and systematic phonic approach. So the great debate on reading method goes on and will continue for a long time yet, if the hundreds of articles on this topic that are published each year can be taken as any kind of yardstick. These approaches to teaching reading to hearing children have also been implemented to some extent with deaf children, but without any great success. If we have learned one thing from our experience with these approaches, it is: Though one approach may work well with some deaf children, no single approach is successful with all deaf children.

Recognizing that there is no failsafe method for teaching reading, schools presently attempt to develop individual reading programs for each child, where the type of instruction and the reading material will depend on the level, interest, and ability of each particular learner. Briefly, the three main practices are

1. Bottom-up models, where the reader first identifies letters, then syllables, then words, and finally ends up at the top with comprehension. This approach holds that meaning resides in the text, and in order to access meaning, the reader has to decode the words.
2. Top-down models place heavy emphasis on the reader's prior knowledge that allows him to make inferences and predictions of the text's meaning and proceed downward to the words in order to confirm old hypotheses or to generate new ones.
3. Interactive models, where reading is seen as a dynamic interaction between reader and text. This active process requires a combination and coordination of both bottom-up and top-down models and is sometimes referred to as balanced reading.

Most would agree that the ability to visually recognize letters and words effortlessly and automatically leads to fluency and comprehension. But reading is more complex than this. Not only is the learner required to recognize words by decoding printed symbols into sounds, but also he must learn to extract meaning from the words and grammar from the text. He also has to learn to make inferences; to sort out what is implied but not stated; and to store, organize, and recall this information. These components of effective reading are enhanced considerably when a reader has an extensive experiential background to help him acquire these skills.

Reading is a complex and formidable task for any child, and for a deaf child it can be overwhelming. Among other things, reading requires a child to decode phonetically based words—a process that is drastically hindered if a child cannot hear the sounds associated with words. It also demands that he use his own command of the spoken language (i.e., English) to help him understand inferences, hidden meanings, idioms, reading between the lines, and much more. Yet, many deaf children, at the very same time as they are learning to read, are asked to use reading as a means of learning English. Herein lies a catch-22.

Reading

Reading is an activity in which one follows a sequence of letters, symbols, or characters arranged in a particular order (left to right in English) and translates them into words, phrases, and sentences that have meaning for the individual. The goal is to comprehend the material and use it for one's needs. Reading activities can vary from a first-grader struggling with simple active declarative statements in a picture book (e.g., *Sarah walked to the park*) to a fourth-grader enjoying a story, from a seventh-grade student doing his best to understand a poem to a father following directions to assemble a barbeque, from a mother following a recipe for a culinary delight to a scholar poring over a learned dissertation. This range is so large that it has been said that reading is the one experience that can present people with the amassed thoughts and experiences of innumerable minds.

There is also an ongoing debate as to when children should start to learn to read. In 1964, Glenn Doman observed that severely brain-damaged children as young as three could be taught to read. Later, his book *How to Teach Your Baby to Read* (1975) became a hot item in parenting literature. In the years that followed, early reading in children has become somewhat of a family status symbol, and parents exchange many tall, if not wild, tales about their child's reading ability. Perhaps it was this parental desire for their children to read at an early age that contributed to the popularity of the TV show *Sesame Street*. Experienced preschool teachers tell us that nearly all of today's toddlers seem to know a lot more about letters and sounds than preschoolers did a generation ago.

In reality, children come to school with about as many different reading levels as there are children. Some will already have begun to read. This may be due to the spread of preschool classes, the use of computer software programs, reader-friendly children's TV programs, and by far and away the most important factor of all—the reading aloud done by the parents. On the other hand, there will be some children who will arrive with little or no reading skills at all; yet these children may blossom into late readers at the age of nine or ten and perhaps go on to achieve reading levels that place them at the top of their class.

To return to the question of when children learn to read, we only have to remember that each child develops at a different physical, emotional, and intellectual rate to discover that there is but one answer—it depends on the child. Children will vary greatly in the age at which they are ready to encounter printed language and learn to read. Hence, to develop a successful reading program, it was not unexpected that schools would take an individual approach to reading instruction. In fact, individualized educational programs have long been the cornerstone of programs for deaf children and children with other disabilities, and teachers of deaf children have long recognized the importance of allowing their students to progress in reading at their own rate. The only strategy that is more important than individualized reading programs is the effort made to ensure that children's experiences with the written word are always positive and rewarding.

Do not think that teachers expect deaf children to show up for the first day of school already knowing how to read. But do know that if children come to class eager to learn and show a real interest in books, then they are likely going to get the most out of reading instruction by their teachers. The goal for the parents of young deaf children therefore should be to plan experiences around the house that will get their deaf child interested in and excited about reading. There are many ways to do this, but four basic principles can serve as a guide.

1. Ensure that books are available and that they are cherished.
2. Become a good reading model for your child.
3. Read to and with your child as often as you can.
4. Encourage children to use reading and writing activities when they are playing or have time on their hands.

Throughout this chapter and the next, we talk about how these principles can be implemented.

The overriding goal is for deaf children to enjoy reading at each stage of their progress towards becoming efficient readers. We want them to enjoy looking at picture books, having someone read to them, reading on their own quietly in a room, going to the library, discussing what they have read in the newspaper, looking up words in a dictionary, drawing, and writing. If you can enable your child to find a passion for reading, this will work wonders for his education, his literacy, and his life. This is not to infer that parents should assume the lead in teaching their children to read. That is the job of the teachers. The parents should, of course, want to reinforce what is being taught in class and give lots of encouragement for their child to do well at school. What we do ask of the parents is to let your guidance, attention, and particularly your enthusiasm, influence your child's attitude to reading, especially in the early years.

Finally, we address a concern that many parents have: Why is it today that so many children, deaf and hearing, are not keen readers? The lack of keenness is especially disconcerting given that today's parents have had more schooling and that they have at their disposal a greater number of books, TV programs, and computer software programs dedicated to reading-readiness and reading skills. Because this disinterest in reading may apply even to those who have excellent reading skills, the reasons are difficult to identify; however, we do suggest the following explanation. We know that young children are influenced greatly by the behaviors modeled around them. Their mannerisms, likes and dislikes, eating habits, posture, and the way they walk and talk will generally portray what they have observed in their own home. The same is true for their attitude toward literacy. The way children feel about reading and writing will usually reflect the way their parents feel about these skills. Parents who read often to their children in an enjoyable fashion and who themselves read a great deal for pleasure are likely to have children who do the same things.

Reading and Deaf Children

Historically, the written word was seen as a more static form of the English language for deaf children than the more transient patterns of the spoken word. Pioneers in education of deaf children believed that since a profoundly deaf child had minimal access to auditory language (because of his inability to hear speech sounds adequately), reading could be used as a concrete means of representing what he was missing in speech. In this way, the child would be able to bypass audition and spoken language and thus acquire English through reading and writing. In theory, it all sounds pretty simple and straightforward: Deaf children would hear through reading and speak through writing. Even brilliant men like Thomas Gallaudet and Alexander Graham Bell would have a deaf child read books to learn the language rather than have him learn the language to read books. Like the early teachers of deaf children, they too thought written characters and ideas could be connected without the intrusion of speech.

Yet, experience with teaching reading to hearing children has shown that reading is not primarily a visual process but is founded on an auditory-based language that integrates both visual and auditory data. Moreover, hearing children are not required to read a language until they can already speak it and have a good knowledge of its vocabulary and grammar. This knowledge helps them anticipate, make sense of, and predict the sequence of information coded in written language. But with deaf children, the subordinate role of reading to language is too often ignored. As a result, deaf children are often required to read in order to develop language. They are being required to learn to read, and to read to learn, both at the same time. This is the "catch-22" to which we have already referred.

The Importance of Communication to the Task of Reading

Let us review the task on hand for deaf children learning to read.

- Reading is the decoding of written symbols that represent language and cognitive structures already possessed by the reader.
- A deaf child will have great difficulty in making sense of what has not been experienced and stored in the form of language.
- Reading can lead to new learning, but the new ideas must be presented in already known words, phrases, and sentences.
- If there are too many new words or phrases, the deaf child's language base will not be able to sustain reading, and frustration will ensue.

Thus, there is little argument that the more language a deaf child brings to the task of reading, the better prepared he will be to learn to read (Brady and Shankweiler 1996). Language also grows from experiences with communication, and reading and writing are just other forms of communication, so whatever a parent can do to facilitate communication in day-to-day interactions will contribute to their deaf child's ability to communicate in print.

Phonological Processing

In recent years, a lot of attention has been given to phonological processing and phonemic awareness, which involve the connection of spoken language to writing or print. Hearing children discover that letters correspond to sounds and use this knowledge when learning to read. This is not meant to imply that reading is a simple matter of attaching meaning to print. As we saw earlier, knowledge about spoken language involves not only phonology but also morphology, syntax, semantics, and the interaction among all of them. All of these aspects have roles to play in the development of reading.

The question now arises: How can deaf children acquire a phonological system when they have a restricted knowledge of spoken language due to their hearing loss? In attempts to answer this question, the research is equivocal. Studies suggest that some good deaf readers seem to have access to phonology, whereas other good readers do not. Overall, there are insufficient data to show whether a deaf child needs phonological processing to learn to read or whether he acquires phonological processing because he has learned to read.

Speechreading as a Route to Phonological Processing

It has been suggested that speechreading could provide phonological information to the deaf child, but this is doubtful. We have long known that speech does not produce sufficient visually distinguishable elements. We saw earlier that groups of sounds produced in the same place were visually identical. Others were not readily visible because of tongue position or coarticulation. Still other features such as intonation, voicing, nasality, and pitch also cannot be seen, and some vowels with similar lip rounding or lip spread can be easily confused. Although there is no question that speechreading provides some phonological information, the amount provided may be insufficient to provide a foundation for learning to read.

Spelling and Fingerspelling as a Route to Phonological Processing

It has also been suggested that spelling might be a means of providing a visual-motor storage for phonology. Spelling can occur in one of three ways: (1) speech; (2) fingerspelling; and (3) writing. Both fingerspelling and writing are unambiguous in their representation of phonemes (they both give one-on-one representation of text), but no evidence has been found that links spelling with learning to read.

Signing as a Route to Phonological Processing

The link between sign language and reading is still in need of investigation, but we do know that deaf children of deaf parents learn a signed language similar to the way hearing children of hearing parents learn a spoken language. The question is, does this early acquisition of language help deaf children learn to read? American Sign Language (ASL) has no written form hence the transition from sign to reading English may present special problems. Nevertheless, it is possible to match most ASL signs with their English word counterpart. This matching could permit a means for the phonological coding of English (Wilbur 2000).

Earlier, we discussed English-based signing, which is the coding of English in signs. We pointed out that there were several sign systems specifically developed for coding English and that two of the most popular were Signing Exact English (SEE) and Signed English. Both systems attempt to code as much of the English language as possible. We also noted that contact signing was another type of English signing that combines ASL signing and some of its features with English word order, and as such, is a convenient means of signing and more readily learned than the formal English sign systems. Because these codes (English signing and contact signing) are isomorphic with printed English at both the morphological and syntactical levels, in theory, they could provide direct exposure to English.

It would appear then that both ASL and English-based signing might be suited for developing sign-based word recognition skills, which may act as a substitute for phonological processing. Hopefully, future research will provide guidance in this respect.

Multiple Routes to Phonological Processing

It is possible that phonological processing by deaf children could result from multiple coding strategies. In other words, varying combinations of fingerspelling, ASL, English signing, writing, speechreading, and speech may work together to provide deaf children with the tools necessary to decipher the printed word (Musselman 2000).

It is unfortunately true that we do not yet fully understand how deaf children learn to read.

Morpheme-Based Processing

Paul (1998) suggested that a visually oriented approach would be more appropriate for teaching deaf children to read. Instead of phonemes (sounds), the written or printed form of a morpheme (the smallest unit of meaning) could be used in a morphographical approach. This system in English is not only visible but also segmental and predictable. The ability to decode words with more than one morpheme, such as in-vis-ible, pre-dict-ing, con-vert-ible-s, requires a knowledge of basic English root words, inflectional suffixes (*-ing, -s, -ed, -er, -ly, -y,* etc.), derivational affixes (*pre-, re-, im-, un-,* etc.), and suffixes (*-ment, -ible, -ful, -tion,* etc.).

In a morpheme-based reading program, children would be instructed in breaking up words, phrases, and sentences into segments. Although this is primarily a visual task, the use of residual hearing, speechreading, and sign could also increase the awareness of morphemic elements. It is thought that instructional material such as morphographically controlled readers and specific exercises could be developed to improve word recognition, decoding, and comprehension skills. It is true that morphographic analysis will not account for all the words in the text, but this approach is worthy of consideration because it could increase word-identification skills.

Which Route to Reading?

This is not a question that anyone but you as a parent can answer. Whichever route you choose when communicating with your deaf child, the key to reading will remain the same: language learning and early exposure to language in whatever input that has been chosen. This input may be signs, speech, or both, depending upon how receptive a deaf child is to the input and how efficient their parents are at using the chosen input. Thus, if deaf children are to experience success in learning a language effectively and then transfer their language skills to reading, they will need

1. Early exposure to a language (and the input can be speech, sign, or both)
2. An optimal language environment (with many opportunities for communication)
3. Proficient language role models
4. Parents who provide them with positive encouragement
5. Parents who expect them to learn language and become literate

Reading Begins at Birth

Language acquisition begins in the home—it is the parents' responsibility to see that language comes to deaf children from as many sources and in as many forms that these children can receive. A decision about the type of communication to use with a deaf child should be made at as early an age as possible, because the first five years are crucial for a child's acquisition of language. This is because of the rapid physical, intellectual, and emotional developments that occur during these years. The child comes into the world quite helpless and fragile, and in order to survive, he needs food and warmth. He also needs some other basic ingredients, and the most important of these is love. Parents certainly need no urging to love their child. Cuddling him from the day of birth seems to be an instinctive reaction, and it is not long before parents demonstrate loving care in hundreds of different ways. All of this has a remarkable impact on his development, because when a child has loving, dependable parents, he will thrive.

But love is not enough. All children must have interesting things to do and should be exposed to a widening range of experiences as they grow. Neither of these tasks is very difficult. Just about anything you do with your deaf child or any place you take him (the supermarket and other stores, the park, the swimming pool, the neighbor's house, the gas station, around the block, etc.) will stimulate his curiosity and give him some further knowledge of the world. Trips can be organized to such out-of-the-ordinary places as the aquarium, museum, zoo, library, business district, farming community, and so forth.

In the early years, toys are major tools for learning. Often it is the simplest toy, or even the box in which the toy came, that does the best job of getting the child's imagination to work. The old standbys of balls, blocks, stackable cups and rings, crayons, construction paper, glue, buttons, safety scissors, rag books, washable markers, peg boards, and simple puzzles will provide a wholesome learning environment for most toddlers. An additional treasure chest consisting of an old trunk or box filled with discarded costume jewelry and clothing, such as dresses, shirts, hats, scarves, shoes and the like, will provide the props for much imaginative play. Books are also excellent items to stuff into chests and keep in a child's room. See the box titled "Oink, Oink Went the Pig," for a story of how one girl's fascination with pigs led to her interest in reading.

Once a positive environment is established, parents can demonstrate, primarily by example, that they value learning. It cannot be said too often that your own reading and writing are the most powerful indicators of your attitude and values; and that these will have more influence on your deaf child than any demands you make of him to engage in similar activities. Second, your excitement and real joy over his achievement also send a very strong message. Enthusiasm is contagious. It almost seems as if a child is programmed to imitate his parents, and because he constantly emulates what he observes, the parents unknowingly are continually teaching him by example. This imitation helps the child to shape his behaviors and aspirations so much so that some people see teaching by example as the most important kind of teaching that the child will ever have. During these preschool years, there are a great many skills, ideas, and even facts that parents can impart to their children, but the most important of all is a love of reading. If, during the preschool years, parents do nothing else but get their deaf child excited about books and reading, the dividends will be great. The old adage "Readers make readers" has been proven over and over again. The search for knowledge and literacy itself stems from reading and is nurtured by it. It doesn't matter if it is the name on a cereal box, the

Oink, Oink Went the Pig!

Elizabeth loved being read to, and almost every evening through her preschool years, her parents read a book to her. She never tired of this nighttime activity, and it reached the point where she wouldn't go to sleep unless a book was read. During these times reading, her Dad would often try to get her to read a word on a page. But this was not to be. She tried at first and then grew frustrated with being asked, telling her Dad, "No. You read it. I want you to read the book. I can't read." In time, her parents came to realize that Elizabeth just wasn't going to be an early reader. But she never tired of being read to and developed a strong liking for picture books about farm animals. She was especially excited about books that had patterns in their story lines. By the time Elizabeth was in kindergarten, she had amassed a considerable collection of farm animal books. Then one day, her Dad asked her to read along with him from a book about the sounds on a farm. Having had this book read to her for so many nights, Elizabeth was able to read along with considerable ease, reciting almost all of the lines from memory. Over the next few days, they read the book again and again, and each time her Dad would ask her to point out some of the animal words they were reading. He never pushed these requests too far for fear that Elizabeth would get frustrated and reject the shared reading activity. The strategy was particularly effective when she was asked to search for words relating to pigs, which happened to be her favorite animal and the theme of her bedroom collection. After this initial foray into word identification in a book with a familiar story, Elizabeth took a greater interest in finding words for farm animals in other books and began attempting to read aloud lines after she had heard the book read a few times. She kept all of her books about farm animals on a shelf in her room separated from other books that belonged to the family.

label on a can, a logo for a gas company, a comic, a story in a book, or whatever, our best advice to parents is: Read to your deaf child, read in front of your deaf child, and read with your deaf child.

What Parents Can Do to Encourage Reading

The American Academy of Pediatrics strongly recommends that children not be encouraged to watch television before the age of two years. We, too, feel that the parents should carefully monitor the amount of time watching TV as well as the time spent playing computer games and surfing the Internet. Despite the amusement, awareness, and skills that these electronic media might impart, they should not be allowed to interfere with parent-child communication or to steal too much time away from reading and writing. Television caters to short attention spans and immediate gratification. Some educators claim that the TV channel-changing and Internet-surfing mindsets common today can promote in children a mental lethargy that is not conducive to good learning habits.

We're not suggesting that electronic media are bad educational tools. One has to learn to use them sensibly, and it would be wise for parents to establish, as early as possible, some form of routine and rules for watching TV, playing computer games, and surfing the Internet. For example, one family of four school-age children made the following rules:

1. No watching TV from Sunday evening to Friday evening during school days
2. No time on the computer until all homework and household chores are completed
3. No chatting on-line, and no phone calls after 9:00 p.m. on school days

The results that this family desired—more time spent reading, playing, and talking among the family—took about one year to realize. The habits that the children had previously developed were hard to break, but after three years, the family was able to lighten up on all of their rules because new habits, especially reading, had developed.

From Bedtime Stories to Shared Reading

Let's take a look at some of the things that those deaf preschoolers, who have been consistently read to at home, have learned that will enhance their reading skills. They learned that

- Sharing a book is a pleasant and satisfying experience.
- Books have fronts and backs, beginnings and endings.
- Favorite books have the same enjoyable stories time after time.
- Stories can have new words and new ideas.
- Other words can be used to help students comprehend a book's words and phrases.
- Signs can be used in a variety of ways to bring meaning to the words on a page.
- They can ask questions and talk about the stories.
- Reading is an experience that can be shared with others.

It is not that these deaf children have received specific reading instruction from their parents; rather they have learned these things merely through the reading experience without any pressure whatsoever being placed on them.

Generally, a complete story is read to foster understanding and enjoyment so that the child will want it read to him again and again. One of the main premises of bedtime story reading is that deaf children can enjoy material that they cannot yet read themselves. Another is that through repeated reading of a story, they will remember much of it and come to enjoy reading it themselves.

Interestingly, the bedtime story reading that parents, deaf and hearing, have been doing for years is something that schools have emulated in one form or another. Lately, one variation of this has come to be known as "Shared Reading," which is a technique that is modeled, in part, on the way bedtime stories are read to youngsters. In this respect, there are several guidelines that a teacher will follow to help students get the most from the learning experience and to ensure that teacher and students interact with the print, the pictures, and with one another. According to the philosophy of Shared Reading, reading should be a pleasant affair, detached from performance demands and criticism, and guided by the skill and intuition of the reader.

Shared Reading is now used in many classrooms where the evolved process involves reading a big book over and over again on successive days with an interactive emphasis arranged by invitations to the students to join in and read along.[1] Students can also role-play sections of the story and, when capable, read independently and/or write their own versions of the story. In some cases, written retellings of stories by older deaf students have indicated that they learned some English from the text signed in ASL.

How To Read a Book to Your Young Deaf Child

In the two sections below, we describe how parents can read books to their young deaf child. These strategies are aimed at children seven years old and under who are unable to read on their own. Although one section looks at reading books orally and the other describes how to read books in signs, you should read both sections because many of the ideas are valid for all methods.

Oral Reading

Following are some suggestions for orally reading a book to your deaf child:

1. If your child is able to hear clearly with the use of hearing aids or cochlear implants, then sit your child on your lap or close to your side so that you can both clearly see the book in front of you.
2. If your child relies on speechreading, then seat him to the side so that he is across from and facing you. Place the book at a 45-degree angle between you and the child.
3. Talk about the book first. Just a few sentences should be enough.
4. Read the book aloud using a clear voice. Vary the tone of your voice as you read so that he can learn to recognize changes in voice patterns with changes in characters.
5. When the child is young, do not be concerned about comprehension. Concentrate on the experience of reading and the es-

tablishment of a routine. See what books your child tends to enjoy the most.

6. Relate the pictures to the story. Point to pictures when they are specifically mentioned in the story.

7. Relate print to the pictures and to words that are spoken.

8. As your child comes to know the story, have him read along as best he can. Allow him to make mistakes. Do not use reading time as a time to correct speech. Because you want to nurture within your child a love for reading, make this time a pleasant experience.

9. As the child becomes older and acquires sufficient speech skills, use reading time as an opportunity to talk about words and phrases. See which words he does not understand and explain them.

10. As the child progresses, he will reach a point when he can read to you. At first, this might be a book that he has memorized. Eventually, the books he reads will be new ones.

Take your child to the library and have him select the books you will read to him. Make the library experience a rewarding one too. Do not have him select a book if you are in a rush. You want your child to learn to browse through books—looking at pictures, finding words in titles that he can recognize, reading a sentence or a page to see if he likes the writing style. All of this will help him feel comfortable being in a library.

Reading in Signs

The following description of how to read books in signs was derived, in part, from the Shared Reading project at the Laurent Clerc National Deaf Education Center at Gallaudet University. The Shared Reading project focuses on ASL as the sign language of choice when reading a book. But many of their suggestions are also applicable to reading books in English signs.

1. Position your child so that he can see your face, your signs, and the book clearly.

2. If you are using ASL, then translate the story to ASL. There are different ways to translate a story for children, two of which are storytelling and story reading. With very young deaf children, it is helpful to start off by using books to engage in *storytelling*, which allows the signer to exercise freedom with the printed story and to use signs and sentences that she knows the child will understand. Parts may be left out and the length of the story shortened to ensure that it is told within the limits of a child's attention span. With *story reading*, a reader translates a story so that it is true to the original text. For example, there are many different versions of popular stories, such as *Little Red Riding Hood* and *The Little Mermaid*. When translating one of these stories, the reader attempts to keep the story similar to the way the author told it.

3. If you are reading in English then, as with ASL, you have the option of storytelling or story reading. In both cases, you use the English signs of your choice. Signing a story in English can be difficult because you are not able to sign as rapidly as you can speak, and it requires a lot of fingerspelling for words that have no sign equivalent. Practice-signing a story first will help you communicate more fluently with your deaf child and make the story more interesting to listen to.

4. Keep the signing and the text visible. The child should be able to see you as well as the book. Articulate your signs and finger-spelling clearly.

5. Allow the deaf child and yourself to interrupt the story to ask questions and to talk about the story and the pictures. After all, an important technique for reading books to young children is to read the same book over and over again. If you do this, then the interruptions allow both the reader and the child to gain more from the stories.

6. Help the child understand the nuances, idioms, invented words, and meaning of the story. We do this with young hearing children too. It might take a bit longer to explain to a deaf child, but the explanation is a part of the process that the child must go through in order to become a reader. Not all English

words are readily translatable to ASL, and some words will require that a signer fingerspell the word or invent a sign. Some
Dr. Seuss books such as *There's a Wocket in My Pocket!* are particularly challenging to read in ASL and in English.

7. Be creative and dramatic in your use of signs. Read the story
beforehand and decide whether you are going to use a storytelling or a story-reading technique. Then think through how
you will read the story to ensure that your signing style is not
only appropriate for the story but also for the age of your deaf
child. For example, you might want to sit a very young child
on your lap as opposed to in front of you, and just sign a few of
the words in the book. If a book is humorous, then this should
be reflected in your manner of signing. If a book is sad, then
the sadness should be obvious from your facial expressions.
Adopt a character in your manner of signing. To do this, you
have to imagine yourself as this character and then become
this person. You can always find books where this can be
done quite easily, as is shown in these few lines taken from
Walking with Mama by Barbara White Stynes:

> The wind blows the cattails in the marsh and pushes Mama's hair
> against my cheek. I laugh because it tickles. Mama talks to me
> about the things we see and find. I rest my head on her shoulder.
> I can smell the pine trees.

In this story, the child is riding in her mother's backpack for a
walk through the countryside. As a reader, you could feel the
wind blowing and the hair brushing against your cheek, which
makes you laugh. You could point to pictures in the book and
ask your child what he thinks the mother might talk about. Pre-
tend to be resting your head on someone's shoulder, taking a
deep breath, and smelling the pine trees. Storybooks for children are written to stimulate the imagination, which makes it
much easier for readers to assume the role of the story's narra-
tor or one of the characters in the story.

8. Involve your deaf child in the actual reading. This can begin at
any age. At the youngest age, involvement can begin with the

child signing a word that is repeated often throughout the book. For example, phrases are frequently repeated in Dr. Seuss's *Green Eggs and Ham,* such as:

> I do not like green eggs and ham. I do not like them, Sam-I-am.
>
> Would you like them in a house? Would you like them with a mouse?
>
> I would not, could not with a goat!
>
> I do not like them in a house. I do not like them with a mouse.

You might start with your child signing HOUSE and then adding the sign MOUSE. Then BOX, FOX, GOAT, BOAT, and so forth. At the beginning, you will likely have to cue your child as to when the sign should be made. One cue your deaf child might recognize is a slowing of the sign: You purposefully make direct eye contact with your child just before tilting your head forward, at which point your child would make the sign HOUSE.

When the child is beginning to read, you can take turns reading passages, with the bulk of the passages initially being yours and then gradually increasing the amount that your child reads. Try this activity with the same book so that your child is familiar with the words and has the confidence to read aloud. If you are translating stories to ASL, a younger child will have to rely on memorizing your translation. However, as the child begins to read, he will be able to offer his own reading of a passage.

9. Use the stories to expand upon ideas and introduce new concepts. Daily reading doesn't have to mean consistent reading every single day. Doing this would require a Herculean effort on the part of the reader and the child. Pitfalls abound in daily reading. Parents might rush through a book just so their children can go to sleep. The parent or the child might nod off during the reading, or frustration can result if the child doesn't understand the story or the parent is unable to sign it. Diversifying the activity from time to time will help curb some of these pitfalls. Be imaginative in how you talk about things during reading time.

For example, the following discussion might take place when reading *The Little Engine that Could*:

Father: Look at this train engine. Have you ever seen a train that looks like this?

Child: No.

Father: What do train engines look like?

Child: [Uses ASL to describe the shape of a train engine.]

Father: Very good. You described that train engine perfectly. Now, what's different about this little engine? [Points to the picture.]

Child: [Points to the smokestack.] It's small.

Father: Yes. It has a smokestack and it's small. It's a picture of how train engines looked a long time ago.

Whenever a child is reading, there are always opportunities for discussion. You can also ask the child to predict what will happen next in the book, act out a part, answer a question that was asked by a character in the book, and so forth. See the box titled "There's More to Reading than Meets the Eye," to learn about how one mother used reading as a means of comparing life long ago with today's lifestyle.

10. Read books simply for the sake of reading books. Above all, let's not forget that the purpose of reading books, especially bedtime reading, is for pleasure. The deaf child has to love watching you read to him.

Story reading and storytelling are not just more opportunities to practice your signing, these are times to introduce new signs to your child, explain concepts, and do many of the other things described above. Reading a book also gives him an opportunity to relax before going to sleep, to feel the comfort of your body, and to know that there is a time during the day when he is alone with you. It might even be a time when a child feels safe in talking about other things. Let the child's mood and reactions to your reading guide the schedule. After all, there are 365 days in a year; time for plenty of

There's More to Reading than Meets the Eye

We do not read simply to find out what an author has to say or how a story is told or to look at pictures. True, this is the way we read most of the time as children, but it would be difficult for a child to develop a passion for reading if this was all that reading was about. Luckily, reading also provides a good springboard for talking about other things in life, many of which relate to what is being read. Donna Venturini describes how her deaf daughter's interest in history led her to buy *The Little House in the Big Woods* and *Farmer Boy*, stories that took place around the time that our not-so-distant ancestors were making a life for themselves. Venturini (2000) described how she and Meghan would read these stories together and veer off to talk about things that they found interesting:

> I am interested in genealogy and often talk about my grandparents and how things were different when they were children. This sparked Meghan's interest in history, so we got *The Little House in the Big Woods*. It was a wonderful story. If there were something that was hard to explain, such as using a pig's bladder for a balloon, I would go to the library to find information on pig's anatomy and show Meghan so that she could visualize the idea. We followed the series next with *Farmer Boy*, which had a lot of emphasis on food. So we tried some of the recipes, and to this day, the kids still eat their pancakes with butter and brown sugar for a special treat just like in *Farmer Boy*.
>
> As we read the series, we would pull out maps and follow the trail of the Ingalls family. Each day, we would make various comments about the story. We would talk about how Laura had only one doll, and then we would count how many dolls Meghan had. If I happened to be washing clothes, I would say how happy I was because I did not have to do the wash outside or that I did not have to make my own soap (35).

Everyone has a story to tell when he or she is reading books to their children. All it takes is a healthy imagination and a little time on hand.

reading and plenty of time for you and your deaf child to make each reading experience a special adventure.

Reading Readiness

Presenting deaf children with reading tasks before they are ready to read will only frustrate or antagonize them. Reading skill depends on both environmental and maturational factors and consists of social, cognitive, linguistic, and motor skills that come about through language-oriented activities. Visits, field trips, videos, and selected programs on TV will help broaden deaf children's experiential background. The stories read to them by their parents will help them understand story structure, and repeated readings will help them remember the plot. The language foundation laid by speech and/or sign, together with the parents' own reading behaviors, will help children understand the purpose and meaning of print before they are asked at school to develop sight word skills, knowledge of word structure and phonics, and the use of context in comprehension. There are many matching-and-reading games available for children as young as three years with which they can have fun without any pressure in matching by size, color, and shape or sorting into like groups. Instructive and enjoyable software programs are also readily available. Valuable sources for finding out more about these materials are librarians, kid's bookstores, toy and game stores, teachers, the Internet, and perhaps most important of all, other parents.

Older Deaf Readers

When a deaf child is ten or eleven years old and still in the early stages of becoming a reader, motivation becomes a critical factor. Children for whom reading has become a difficult and threatening experience inevitably have a history of failure, which means they need to have positive and successful reading experiences. It is important then to match the child's language level with the materials to be read, because if the language of the story is beyond his comprehension, then he cannot be expected to read it. Just as important as the reading level is the interest level of the material. A high-interest, low-vocabulary book on airplanes, motorbikes, or cars for an older boy, for example, would most likely be more interesting to him than *The Little Gingerbread Boy* or *The Three Little Pigs.*

Reading material can be divided into several categories—four of which can be labeled as functional, informational, instructional, and recreational—but the lines separating these various types are unclear and permit much overlap.

Functional Reading

One of the best places to start with an older deaf child is with functional reading, which is the application of reading to practical situations that are often of intrinsic interest to the older child because of their close relationship to events in his everyday life. Moreover, it can begin at such an easy level that it gives children the confidence and encouragement they need to pursue other reading activities.

Examples of basic levels of functional reading materials are

- International pictograms at airports (men and women's washrooms, stairs, luggage, food, drink, first aid, arrivals, departures, information, currency exchange, escalator, etc.)
- Corporate logos (Microsoft, Shell, Wendy's, etc.)
- Roadside billboards (places to eat, sleep, get gas, and make telephone calls)
- Road signs (Yield, Stop, Playground, Slippery When Wet, Do Not Enter, Men at Work, School Zone, One Way, Steep Grade, etc.)
- Clothing care symbols (wash, bleach, dryer, iron, dry clean, etc.)
- Safety words (Danger, Beware, Exit, Keep Out, Push, Pull, etc.)
- Street names and local maps
- Fast food menus and prices
- Simple recipes for those who like to cook
- Store names for those who like to shop
- Aisle names in superstores to help find articles
- Air, bus, and train schedules (note: easily obtained on the Internet)

• Labels on food containers
• Shopping lists (for groceries, vegetables, etc.)

Initially, sight words can be taught by demonstration, prompting, and if necessary, repeated practice to ensure that meaning is brought to print. Because many of these words are ubiquitous in our daily lives, they are never in short supply. Here's a four-step plan to help you get started.

Step 1

Identify up to ten functional words that are present in your household. These can be name brands, such as *Sunbeam* (toaster), *Kenmore* (washer and dryer), *Crest* (toothpaste), and *Levi's* (pants); labels, such as *Broil* (oven), *Repeat* (remote control), and *Ice* (refrigerator); or simple instructions and information, such as *60 Watts Only* (light) and *Close tight* (food jar).

Step 2

Use these words when talking about objects and activities.

Take the toast out of the Sunbeam.

Check to see if we have any Crest left.

What temperature is the oven turned to?

Which button on the remote control turns off the sound? What does it say?

Step 3

Have your deaf child identify ten to twenty other functional words in the house. He should write them down in a booklet and then show you where these words are. Every now and again, take your child to these objects and have him read the labels. Do this with your list of functional words too.

Step 4

Repeat this activity using functional words outside of the household.

Informational Reading

Informational reading helps us to gain knowledge, insight, or understanding. Examples of reading material typically associated with this type of reading, which can be used to motivate older deaf children learning to read, are

- Atlases
- Picture dictionaries
- Illustrated encyclopedias
- TV guides (for program information)
- Telephone books
- Newspapers (basketball, football, and hockey scores or the movie schedule)
- Catalogs

It is not difficult to find informational reading materials that are of high interest to children. Use your deaf child's interests to stimulate them to read. Following are examples of what you can do if your child has an interest in one of these activities.

Clothing

Let your child select a particular type of clothing, such as T-shirts and knee-length dresses. Then have your child look up this item in a clothing catalog and record words that are used to describe clothing, such as cotton, polyester, sizes, and color.

Professional Sports

Sports writing ranges from strictly informational ("Capriati won her match in straight sets.") to colorful analysis ("If last night's play is any indication, Johnson will be taking the express train back down to his former double-A farm team."). To enjoy reading about sports, a child must know the vocabulary associated with each sport. Get a rulebook about a particular sport and help your child learn its terminology. Write these words on a card along with a brief explanation or picture. Then point these words out in the newspaper and explain their meaning in sentences.

Instructional Reading

As the name implies, instructional reading tells the reader how to do something. Popular types of instructions include

- Assembly instructions
- Information about how to use a product (e.g., carpet cleaner, stain remover, etc.)
- Recipes
- Medical labels (e.g., 2 tablets 3 times day)
- Rules for games
- Operating manuals (for a washing machine, dryer, dishwasher, toaster, coffeemaker, VCR, TV, lawnmower, microwave oven, and the family vehicle)
- Knitting and sewing instructions

Critical to understanding instructional reading materials is the ability to follow directions. This is something that can be readily done around the house. Try the following activities.

Cooking

Most children enjoy cooking. Many cookbooks contain some simple recipes that even the beginning reader can follow once he has learned the vocabulary associated with measurement and directions (e.g., 6 oz., 2 cups, stir slowly; grate; mix while pouring milk into the bowl).

Writing Notes

Start off by writing simple directions to your child, such as the following.

> Good morning Claire. I will be home at 10:00 a.m. Please feed the cat. Bring in the newspaper.
>
> Love, Mom

Try and plan for someone to be present in case your child does not understand the message. You may want to incorporate into your directions language that is commonly found on prescriptions, directions, and assembly instructions. For example,

> Alex, please water the plants in the den every second day. Use the small watering can. Half-fill it with warm water. Give about one cupful to each plant.
>
> Love Dad.

Also, allow your child to write notes to you and show him how much you appreciate reading them. If he is already using the Internet, use e-mail as one source of directives. If you are in a creative mood, you might try mailing some on a postcard every now and again.

Eventually, you will move from your written directions to having your child read real instructions and following them.

Recreational Reading

Recreational reading is what comes to mind when we think about reading at home. It is reading for pleasure, and these days, it is not difficult to find literature that is of high interest and low vocabulary and is yet suitable for older children. These stories are generally predictive (i.e., they allow the reader to figure out what is coming next) and are generally about events familiar enough to the child for him to use his own experience to help decode the message. The cumulative effect of repetition in the story (as well as repeated readings by the caregiver) helps to extend the child's sight vocabulary, assist in memorization, and enable success and task satisfaction. Older children may feel uneasy about having books read to them, and if this is the case with your deaf child, then let him try reading alone, but make yourself available to answer questions or give help when he asks for it.

There is almost always a continuing need to motivate and interest older children in reading. Low-level reading skills often cause these children to get caught up in a vicious circle. Because of their poor reading skills, they don't read very much or very often, which makes it all the more difficult for them to keep up. It will take time, but with the thousands of titles available in libraries and bookstores, a diligent search is certain to turn up something of interest for him, whether it be a comic book, joke book, or magazine. In addition, contemporary or classical stories written (or rewritten) in a low language level and other material, such as science fiction, mystery, history, fantasy, and realism, are readily available and can be tackled in easy steps when your child is ready.

Attitude Counts

Although words on paper might be difficult for deaf children to read, parents' emotions are not. Deaf children (and all children for that matter) can read your face better than a book. Therefore, maintain a positive attitude about your child's effort in learning to read. Strive for a relaxed atmosphere in which there is no pressure on the child. It is a long and arduous journey from sight word recognition to good reading, and to increase his comprehension, a child will need to learn the appropriate strategies, such as

• Skimming for ideas
• Scanning for information
• Predicting what comes next
• Making use of context to obtain meaning

These processes can be fostered by a wide selection of reading material and frequent discussions about words, phrases, sentences, and their meanings. Always be guided by the child's strengths—his own language, interests, and knowledge.

Finally, do not be fooled by commercials for costly programs that promise immediate remediation of your child's reading difficulties. That there is no quick fix is obvious from the current standards in the United States and the long history of unresolved arguments on how best to teach reading to both deaf and hearing children. In spite of all the research and the hundreds of books and the thousands of articles on the subject, reading remains the greatest stumbling block to the acquisition of an education and to literacy itself. If you accept this fact, it will be much easier for you to find the time and summon the effort to help your deaf child gain a love for reading.

Twenty-Five Great Reading Strategies

Over the years, we have listened to parents of deaf children tell us what helped them when their child was learning to read. These ideas number in the hundreds and range from "Just give your child lots of love" to "Buy a phonetic reading program." What we have done is put together twenty-five of the best ideas that we have heard.

1. Set time aside every single day to read to your child.
2. Talk and/or sign with him about what he is reading.
3. Use puppets to roleplay a story.
4. Have white boards and washable markers placed in key areas (kitchen and his bedroom) to help in communication.
5. For preschool children, write family names on homemade place cards.
6. For preschool children, develop a daily diary with stick figures and one or two words describing what that figure did. For example, "went shopping" or "swimming."
7. Start a family journal and read it to the family at regular intervals.
8. Encourage the use of TTY and e-mail.
9. Reread the stories he likes over and over again.
10. Set a time when everybody in the family reads.
11. Play lots of word games appropriate to his age and interests, such as *Concentration, Junior Scrabble, Pictionary,* etc.
12. Meet his teacher and ask how you can help with his reading skills at home.
13. Use a picture dictionary.
14. Supply books that complement work being done at school.
15. Use photographs to make a book about your child's experiences (e.g., a holiday, beach picnic, birthday party, or trip to a farm). In lower-case script, print a simple story line underneath each picture.
16. Search the Internet for games involving language and motor skills.
17. Encourage a study of word origins (an etymological dictionary will prove a big help for parents).

18. Obtain software on reading activities for your personal computer.
19. Have age-appropriate books in every room.
20. Review homework assignments and make sure your child understands what he is being asked to do.
21. Go on walks with him to discover plants, insects, birds, trees, etc., in your local area.
22. As he gets older, discuss the headline news with him.
23. Sign and/or sing nursery rhymes and children's songs with him.
24. Label everything in the house with flash cards.
25. Have magnetic alphabet letters on the fridge to spell out his name and other words he wants to know.

Now, can you add five more to this list?

Conclusion

For deaf children, the various approaches to teaching reading (bottom-up, top-down, and interactive) have all been tried but with varying results (Yurkowski & Ewolt 1986). We know that one approach will work well with some deaf children but not with all. There is also no right age to begin reading, and today, school programs permit children to progress at their own rate. The major aim for parents is not to dabble with instruction but rather to ensure that their deaf child develops a real interest in books and a genuine excitement about reading. The basic ways to achieve this goal are

• ensure that books are available and cherished
• become an excellent reading model
• read to, for, and in front of your child whenever you can, and
• encourage him by using reading and writing in as many activities as possible

Notes

1. Shared Reading with deaf children evolved in the late 1980s, when Dutch investigators reported on a special course that they had designed to

teach hearing parents how to read and tell stories in sign language to their deaf children. In the early 1990s, David Schleper from the Clerc Center at Gallaudet University piloted the Shared Reading Project in Hawaii. Using his observations on how deaf parents and deaf teachers read to deaf students, Schleper developed a list of fifteen strategies for reading effectively to deaf children. Then he trained deaf persons how to work with hearing families of deaf students. These deaf tutors went into the homes once a week and taught the hearing parents how to read books to their deaf children by modeling the reading principles and by providing feedback to the parents as they practiced their new skills. Subsequently, long-distance video conferencing technology was used to communicate with the target audiences. Shared Reading Bookbags are also available, which are designed to teach parents, caregivers, and teachers how to read to deaf children using ASL and how to use the strategies enumerated above to make book sharing most effective. Each bag contains an individual storybook (there are five sets of ten in the series), a videotape of the story in ASL, an activity card for fun ideas related to the story, and a bookmark with tips for reading.

CHAPTER 8

Writing

This chapter will help you understand

- That writing is more than written speech and is related to reading
- The first steps in writing begin in the home
- The roles of handwriting, punctuation, and spelling in shaping a child's overall writing style
- Some strategies to help your child write better

Writing, like reading, improves with practice. But getting children to write is not as simple as placing a computer keyboard or a pencil and paper in front of them and waiting for something to happen. It might seem logical that the more comfortable people are using words in conversation the better able they should be at writing. But sometimes even the best of speakers and signers are reluctant to write more than the occasional note or e-mail message. Becoming a writer involves motivation and confidence in one's ability to convey messages in print. Following is a story of how one teacher got two deaf children to enjoy writing.

The teacher taught in the middle school program at a school for deaf children and had a twice-weekly writing requirement: Students engaged in fifteen minutes of uninterrupted, sustained, silent writing everyday. During the two writing sessions, the students were encouraged to write about anything at all, and the teacher read what they wrote but made no corrections to their work. Instead, he would meet with the students individually in brief encounters that often led to animated discussions. The teacher helped the students think about what they had written, how best to get the message across, and how they might improve upon their efforts the next time they wrote.

Heather was a twelve-year-old deaf girl with a fifth-grade reading level whose English skills were adequate at a basic level. She could write grammatically correct sentences following patterns that her previous teachers had taught her. She kept her stories short and her grammar accurate. This manner of writing, however, lacked vitality, and at the beginning of the year, she often rendered dry recaps of her life:

> Saturday, I had a lot of fun. I went to see the movie called, *The Princess Diaries*. I enjoyed the movie. It was a fun movie to watch. I stayed home Sunday. I watched TV with my sister.

Through conversations with the teacher, she realized the value of elaborating upon different aspects of her story. In addition, she came to understand that one function of writing is to entertain other people. She learned that writing a story is not simply telling something to somebody; rather, it is saying something to others in such a way that they will want to read it. At first, Heather found this a difficult concept to incorporate into her thinking about writing. For years, she had aimed at writing correctly and with precision rather than for social reasons. To write well, she now had to learn how to take risks in her writing by experimenting with words and letting the story, rather than her knowledge of grammar, guide her writing.

By the middle of the school year, Heather's writing was noticeably different. Her stories grew in length, and her sentences increased in complexity. She also came to enjoy watching her teacher's reactions to the things that she wrote:

> Who would have thought that a visit to my aunt's place would be so exciting. She is really a very boring person and I dreaded going there because there is nothing to do. I usually watch TV or sit around until it is time to go home. But yesterday, my aunt's dog gave birth to triplets. I was there to see the whole thing. They were so cute. . . .

And off she went writing. Her written stories were not always in good form grammatically, but they were alive and brought her much pleasure.

Boyd was a sixteen-year-old deaf boy who read at a first-grade level and had little interest in school. He started the year writing one or two sentences during the writing period, none grammatically correct and seldom did they make any sense. Early attempts to talk about what he had written were fruitless, and for about two months, the writing period remained a trying time for both Boyd and the teacher. Eventually the teacher came to realize that the insecurities in Boyd's home life (he was undergoing a change in foster parents) and his lack of friends around the school were bigger barriers to his writing than his poor command of English. By this point, the teacher had developed a good rapport with Boyd and was able to have long conversations with him outside of the classroom. He then had Boyd write about some of their shared conversations. During his writing, Boyd would recall parts of what they had talked about and would ask the teacher for the English words for the signs they had used in their conversations. This was the turning point. His confidence in writing grew, and by the end of the school year, Boyd was writing up to one-and-a-half pages during the silent writing periods. His grammar was still weak, but his written vocabulary expanded considerably during this time.

What this teacher did in the classroom is something that you, as a parent of a deaf child, can readily do at home. You can do it by fostering a positive attitude toward writing, by rewarding his efforts, and by encouraging him to see writing as another tool for socially interacting with others. There is an old saying that the way a person signs or speaks is a part of who that person really is. Perhaps the same can be said for writing.

The Nature of Writing

For hearing children, the four modes of language—listening–speaking and reading–writing—are closely related. They can be regarded as two interdependent pairs, with the second of each pair being an extension of the first. As with listening and speaking, reading and writing are mutually supportive of each other. If the ability in one declines, so will the ability in the other. They are also interactive in that good readers are generally good writers and good writers are generally good readers, but contrary to popular belief, children do not first learn to read before learning to write. In fact, child development researchers tell us that writing is actually an easier activity for young children to learn than reading. Parents who have witnessed their youngster experimenting with early writing (scribbling) in the most inappropriate places will heartedly agree.

Unfortunately, in the instructional approaches to reading, writing is given a very small role, if any, by those teachers who see reading as a sequence of discrete skills that have to be mastered as a separate language arts subject. We believe that writing, like reading, requires a working knowledge of the phonological system of English (i.e., the alphabetic system and sounds upon which print and script are based), and therefore, we think that reading taught together with writing would most likely accommodate different reading styles. In order to become good writers and readers, students must be taught how to organize their ideas, clarify their thinking, and examine implications derived from the context.

What Is Writing?

Writing is not simply written speech; the ability to write requires skills that go beyond those needed for spoken language. Writing, for example, presupposes at least the following four stages:

- Planning
- Translating ideas into words
- Organizing the content
- Reviewing the output

There are two broad aspects to writing. The first consists of the *product*. This is the resultant message and includes elements, such as the vocabulary, syntax, and mechanics (punctuation, capitalization, and legibility). The second is the *process*, where higher-level skills are required to accommodate aspects, such as intent, audience, organization, and style.

To compose a message, the writer first must go through a series of thought processes that includes determining the structure of the text, choosing the right vocabulary, constructing correct sentences in the proper sequence, and arranging them in paragraphs that convey the major points. He also has to be mindful of spelling, punctuation, and handwriting; all this while keeping in mind what the intended audience knows and what they need to know if the message is to be understood. As with reading, there are some unresolved questions concerning the effects that a deaf child's limited access to phonology will have on the task of writing. Comments made on phonology in the previous chapter on reading also apply to writing.

Deaf students are not the only ones who may find writing to be a challenging task. Studies have shown that the writing of many college-entrance students lacks organization, cohesion, and clarity. In fact, only a minority of these college students was capable of writing a competent persuasive essay or an accurate and precise description of an event. In surveys, many students have reported great difficulty with writing. Even more have claimed that they hated writing at school and that the longer they stayed in school, the more they disliked it. This is disconcerting because writing is seen as the ultimate goal in a communicative process that starts with cognition; moreover, writing stimulates and provides greater accuracy to our thinking.

At a practical level, writing is a skill that all of us, at some time or other, will need because of its indispensable role in our culture. The proliferation of forms that we all have to complete and the growing encroachment of computers as a means of social interaction require that we submit written information on more and more occasions. Whether we use pen or keyboard, writing is a part of our daily lives.

Creating the Right Attitude

At the beginning of this chapter, you were told a story about how a teacher helped his deaf students develop a positive attitude toward writing through twice-weekly short periods of writing. The students selected the topic, and the teacher never corrected their efforts. He did, however, read each story carefully and talked to the students individually about them. Generally, the period of talk was brief—sometimes as short as two minutes. In addition to the content of what had been written, the teacher was interested in the student's perception of how effective they had been in their writing. Indeed, the success of this writing experience was intimately linked to the students learning that writing is another important means of social interaction.

The teacher's approach to this writing activity illustrates six key behavioral characteristics that can foster a love of writing and that incorporate principles that relate to the development of good adult-child interactions. Even more important, they can readily be used in the home by parents to create an environment conducive to writing by their deaf children. If implemented consistently, the following characteristics will help boost deaf children's confidence in their ability to write:

1. Enthusiasm. The teacher showed genuine enthusiasm for all written work, and this provided an extrinsic reward to the students for their writing efforts and encouraged them to take a much greater interest in what they wrote.
2. Acceptance. Everything that was written was accepted. If a student turned in what for him was a below-average performance, then that was accepted without any negative comment. However, if the written work was exceptionally good, then the teacher openly recognized this effort.
3. Self-expression. The teacher always maintained a focus on the goal of the writing activity, which was to have the students engage in self-expression by writing about anything so that they might develop and maintain an interest in writing. Therefore, little or no attention was given to working on specific grammatical or vocabulary tasks during the writing periods.
4. Confidence. The children had no fear of making mistakes. When a child does not have to worry about making mistakes and can concentrate on saying something, writing for him becomes an experiment in which he can try out different strategies for telling a

story as well as explore a variety of ways to manipulate words, phrases, and sentences.

5. Routine. Routine plays an important role in children's learning experiences. The teacher recognized its importance by requiring that his students participate in a free writing activity at regular intervals twice a week throughout the school year. Learning will last longer if it occurs systematically and gives the child frequent opportunities to explore and internalize concepts, acquire automaticity in a skill, and gain an appreciation for what he has learned.

6. Pride. The teacher's comments during his individual conversations with the students about their writing also aimed at instilling in them a sense of pride in their achievements. He did this by offering praise when it was deserved, and more importantly, by sharing with the students what he had learned from reading the stories. Every child likes to know that he can help someone learn, and writing is an excellent vehicle for this purpose.

For hearing people, writing is an important part of their overall communication skills, but it undoubtedly plays an even more important role in the lives of deaf people because there are so many occasions when it helps bridge the communication gap between deaf and hearing. Deaf adults are usually accustomed to carrying a pen and notepad everywhere they go because it allows them to communicate in situations where signing and speaking are not options.

Thus, parents who make writing an important function in their household are, in effect, exposing their deaf child to the varied functions that writing will have for him throughout his life. See box titled "The Writing Board," which describes a simple method for creating an atmosphere that encourages writing in the household.

Write at Home: The Early Years

As with reading, the first step in encouraging a deaf child to write is to set a good example. When a child sees his parents writing, he will become eager to put his own marks on paper. And it is a simple

The Writing Board

When deaf children understand that writing has a valuable function in their lives, they will be more inclined to take an interest in learning to write. For this understanding to take place, they must see other people write and have opportunities to read what other people have written. Both of these experiences will be facilitated if the whole family engages in writing.

A writing board placed in a conspicuous place in the house is an exciting way of getting the family to write. Use the following procedures to get started with your household's "Writing Board."

1. Put up a bulletin board somewhere in your house. You could even post it on your refrigerator door, but make sure it has borders so that it stands out from the other objects on the door, such as magnetic pictures. The board should be small enough that it does not become too cluttered.
2. Be the first person to write a story and place it on the board.
3. Talk to family members to gain their support for this concept.
4. Attach a weekly schedule near the board whereby each family member will take a turn at writing something.
5. Make a list of things that the family can write about, such as

   – Describe a familiar person, such as a family member or friend.
   – Describe a book that you are reading.
   – Describe a good TV program that you recently watched.
   – Write about some of the things that you want to do this week (a great way to teach your children about setting and accomplishing goals).
   – Write a poem, story, or joke.
   – Post a picture and describe why you like it.
   – Post a photograph of a family member, or one that a family member took, and then write about it.
   – Write about something that someone in the family did recently.
   – Write about a dream.
   – Start a letter to someone and ask if the person writing next can finish it.
   – Talk about things that give you lots of pleasure.

6. Ask the members of the family to give ideas about what they would like to see written and placed on the board.

Every now and again, take one of the written works and make it into a screen saver for your computer. This is easily done on any computer with a scanner.

matter to call his attention to the many acts of writing that occur all the time in the home, such as taking down phone messages, making shopping lists, writing a letter, sending an e-mail, writing thank-you notes and birthday and special event cards, writing checks, paying bills, and many other writing experiences. He will eventually come to realize that writing is an essential part of the environment and is a form of communication that fulfills a variety of important functions, such as the conveying and storing of information.

Even toddlers who can barely hold a crayon thoroughly enjoy "writing" all over a sheet of paper, or, if paper is not provided, all across a newly painted wall. Parents should encourage this love of drawing and prevent artistic efforts from appearing on unwanted areas by providing the child with a box of writing materials, including large crayons or washable markers and large sheets of paper. Children will begin to write first by scribbling and then proceed to drawing increasingly accurate representations of letters and words.

A bulletin board, the refrigerator door, or some other prominent location can be used to show the results of his efforts. Displaying his work and talking about it with the child gives him the best reward of all—your interest, encouragement, and enthusiasm. See box titled "In and Out of the Garbage Pail," for a story of a young child who used his imagination to create his own link to writing.

At kindergarten age, your child might draw a picture and "write" a string of five or so squiggles under it with perhaps a letter or a number thrown in, but he will know exactly what his writing says and with very little prompting will "read" it back. He has yet to learn how to hold a pencil, the correct posture for writing, and the direction that writing must take, which in English is from left to

In and Out of the Garbage Pail

Michael hadn't yet turned two years old when he discovered the greatest treasure in his early childhood—the burnable garbage pail. He lived in the country, and his parents had two garbage pails in the kitchen. One was for garbage, as we normally know it to be in most households. The second was an open pail into which paper products were tossed to be burned in an incinerator outside of the house. The pail was positioned in the busiest path in the house; you had to pass it to get to the kitchen, dining room, hallway, family room, den, mudroom, and bathroom. Michael discovered at a very early age that the things that were tossed into the pail were of different shapes, sizes, colors, and textures from what was thrown into the other garbage pail. And with a pair of scissors, crayons, and glue stick, they could be shaped into many more shapes and sizes. When he was a preschooler going to school for just a half-day, he would literally spend hours making things from what he had found in the burnable garbage pail. In time, he began to write on the things he made, and this was his first experience with writing. At first, the writing was gibberish, but it eventually progressed from misspelled, but understandable, words to real words ("I love mom. XX00XX Michael"). Michael gave his paper crafts to his parents and siblings as presents or feel-good messages. Even when he was in the first grade, he would come home from school and go directly to the pail to see if there was anything from which something interesting could be made. With his imagination, there always was. His parents encouraged his writing activity by always showing how much they enjoyed watching him make things from the garbage pail and reading with relish everything that he wrote. Michael is now ten years old, and from time to time, he keeps a daily journal.

right and top to bottom. But nothing seems to contain his desire to draw and copy letters and then words.

Some children at age four or five may lack the fine motor skills required to form anything but scribbles and drawings. This is why encouragement by parents will go a long way to helping him through this stage of development. These days, the computer keyboard and some excellent software can provide youngsters with an enjoyable way to begin learning the mechanics of writing and to pick up other motor skills as well. We do want to emphasize, however, that parents do not need to be overtly concerned about the mechanics of writing. Schools, after all, tend to devote a considerable amount of the curriculum to writing activities.

As with reading, there is no exact timetable as to when a child starts writing letters, phrases, and sentences. Some children starting kindergarten may be able to print their name and more; others may only be able to produce a few letters or drawings. The parents' role is to give the child numerous opportunities to use crayons, pencils, washable felts, the computer keyboard, or any other print-generating instrument, such as old typewriters, which are readily available at little expense in this computer age.

Parents who share books and read stories with their children and who, themselves, read a lot generally have children who love reading. In the same vein, parents who enjoy writing and encourage their child to write may not necessarily be preparing him for a literary career as a reporter, author, novelist, or poet, but they will help their deaf child develop a positive attitude toward writing. Perhaps more than anything else, the right attitude is crucial to opening the mind of the child at some later date, so that he will take a greater interest in developing an understanding of how ideas, words, sentences, and narratives interrelate.

Write at Home: When School Begins

Your involvement in your deaf child's writing does not end with your child getting on the school bus. Teaching writing is a difficult task for teachers, and the more you understand the role of schools in your child's road to learning to write, the better you will be able to help your child write at home.

In the past, there were two extreme, yet popular, approaches for teaching deaf children how to write. The old "hammer the grammar" style of yesteryear concentrated on teaching parts of speech (nouns, verbs, adjectives, adverbs, etc.) and rules of grammar (subject-verb agreement, infinitive as a noun, etc.). At the other end, there is the "free" writing approach with invented spelling and little or no guidance (a.k.a., interference) from the teacher. In between these extremes, some teachers gave out a topic once a week. A certain amount of time was allocated for students to write a composition (ranging from a single sentence to a full-length essay) that was collected by the teacher, who later made corrections with a red pencil and then gave the composition back to the young authors. Some teachers might ask one or more of the writers to come to the front and read their effort to the class. The results obtained with the two extremes and the in-between approaches were, strangely enough, only marginally different from each other, but none of them was very satisfactory. Today, writing is a much more exciting and meaningful affair, where the mark of a good writing program is one that is tailored to each deaf child.

The question you have to ask yourself is this: Now that your child is learning to write at school, what can you, as a parent, do to facilitate writing at home? Later in this chapter, we provide a list of strategies for engaging your child in writing activities in the home; however, at this point, we would like to highlight some basic principles that can help you encourage your deaf child to write.

Characteristics of Early Writing Experiences in the Home

Writing experiences at home can help reinforce the writing instructions that deaf children receive at school. You can begin by providing your child with the tools for writing (pens, paper, computer) and resolving to be positive toward his attempts to write. The next step is to introduce your child to writing activities. These activities should be real ones that have a function in your household, or at the very least, have the appearance of having one. Contrived activities might make your home seem to be too much like school, and you risk turning your child off. Here are some examples of real and contrived writing activities.

Real Writing Experiences

- Shopping lists
- List of things to do

  - Clean up bedroom
  - Put toys in basement
  - Invite Grandma over for dinner
  - Make dental appointment
  - Take the dog for a walk

- Instructions left for someone to do something

  - Jonn. Wash car.
  - Dad. Mom and I went to see Mrs. Tanner. Back at 5:30. Barbeque hamburgers for dinner. Love Anna.
  - Jessalyn. Please go to Brennan's house after supper.
  - Pippa. Remember to take water to soccer practice tonight.

- Things to take on a trip
- Things to do on a trip
- Thank you notes, birthday cards, Christmas cards, etc.
- A note to apologize for doing something wrong
- Fill out a completed subscription form for a magazine
- A letter to say why you should get a certain thing for your birthday

Contrived Writing Experiences

Note that some of these ideas for writing are quite good. However, they are all contrived and should not be the main source of writing experiences in the house unless they are part of a school assignment.

- Write a make-believe story about an elf that moves in with the family.
- Write about what you did at the zoo today.
- Write about what you want to be when you grow up.
- Describe your day at a friend's house.
- Describe what you like to do when you are feeling happy or sad.

The more your child engages in writing experiences that have meaningful goals and are not just being done for the sake of writing, the more likely it is that he will come to enjoy writing.

When creating writing experiences around the house, bear in mind the following six points:

1. *Write about familiar things.* This is especially important during the early years of learning to write. Whether you or your child selects the topic, it is always easier to write about experiences that are very familiar—a guideline that many best-selling authors follow. Typically, the ones that the child selects will be related to real-life events (e.g., shopping with mom, fishing with dad) and people and things they know well (e.g., friends, pets, games).

2. *Provide guidance as needed.* Unlike the learning of words, signs, phrases, sentences, and syntax in conversation, where the child creates his own strategies, the exploration of the printed word in reading and writing often reflects adult influences. Parents usually will point out words on cereal boxes and other packaging, advertisements, newspapers, magazines, storybooks, and the like, which the child combines with his own individual experiences to develop a personal learning style for coping with script. You can provide a list of words your child may choose from, be available to help with the writing if your child should ask, provide a starting sentence if he needs it, or have a conversation in which you can provide some clues that your child may use in his writing.

3. *Be flexible in your expectations.* Accurate spelling, neat handwriting, and correct punctuation may be desirable characteristics, but they are not necessarily features of strong writing skills. Today, keyboarding skills have come to replace handwriting as the preferred writing tool. This is not to deny that handwriting is a valuable skill but rather to suggest that remedial handwriting instruction for young children may not be as important as the attention given to creative aspects, such as planning, organizing, and analyzing their own writing. These are the aspects that really count in the overall development of good writing habits.

4. *Praise your deaf child's strengths.* Praise is always more effective than criticism for reinforcing desirable skills. Be specific and honest in your comments, because false praise is also ineffective. Remember that if a child enjoys writing, he will keep at it; and generally, the more he writes, the better he will become.

5. *Prominently display your child's writing.* Encourage your child's writing efforts by displaying his written work on the refrigerator door, walls, doors, or even a notice board specifically put up for that purpose.

6. *Get the whole family involved in writing.* Here's a truism about our society: Everyone likes to receive things. Presents are great, but a note on the counter, e-mail messages, and a letter slipped under the bedroom door are also appreciated. Make it a family practice to write notes to one another. It doesn't take long, for example, for an older sibling to write a note to a younger deaf sibling.

> Robert, I heard you did well on your math test today. I'm going to try to do better on mine. Love Susan

Put your deaf child in charge of writing down chores for the family (after consulting with you of course).

Isabella, take out the garbage.

Judith, pull weeds.

Everyone. Keep the cat out of the pantry.

Dad, stay out of my room!

Another effective strategy for involving the family in writing is the use of journals. Children generally use these to write about daily happenings or any other topic they wish to record. Made-up stories and other imaginative writings have found their way into many a journal. We have also seen journals that were used to carry out a dialogue between father and child. Because children write more and write better when they have a real audience who is interested and eager to read what is written, the dialogue in the journal approach has much to commend it. One unusual but rewarding venture is described in the box titled, "Open Family Journal."

Open Family Journal

An open family journal is simply a notebook in which each member of the family is free to add any comments they wish. It can be a story about someone else in the family.

"I saw Peter talking to Sarah today. I think he likes her."

"Joni dove head first off a diving board for the first time ever. She landed on her belly and wouldn't do it again."

Or it can be about something that happened at school or work.

"Today I got sent to the office for throwing an eraser. But I didn't throw it. Nina did. But I didn't tell."

"I got permission to take one week off work over the Easter holidays. I am going to take the family on a vacation to see the Ice Hotel in Quebec."

Or it can be a poem, joke, wish list, or anything else. It can be as long or short as a person wants it to be. Everyone in the family is encouraged to write something, with few boundaries for prose other than those for excluding bad language and meanness. Pictures can also be placed in the journal. At some point, the journal can be read back with nostalgia, joy, and apprehension at family get-togethers.

A Word about Invented Spelling

Invented spelling refers to young children's attempts to use their best judgments about spelling (e.g., *kom* for *come, kort* for *caught, difrint* for *different*) as they learn to write. Not only do many educators see invented spelling as a great help to the child wanting to write a message, but they also regard it as an important stage in spelling development because the characteristics of invented spelling change after exposure to standard spelling instruction. See box titled, "Invented Spelling," for examples of how English lends itself to variations in spelling.

Even though some children persist with invented spelling over several years, longitudinal studies show that these children do adapt to standard spelling. Spelling is not always easy because of

Invented Spelling

Der Prinnts,

Wen ur child brings riting home do not be serprized at the speling. Inglsh is confusing for students and insistints that they uz standurd speling can inhibit thair dezir to rite. We wll be using inventd speling in awer riting.

U can hlp by prazing thair wrk and hav them red thair riting to u. No that wen ur chld is mor famillyer with riting he or she will be tort to mak the tranzishun to standurd speling.

Thank U

Teacher

the vagaries of the phonetic relationships and sound-spelling correspondences in the English language. The difficulty is seen, for example, in the pronunciation and spelling of words like, for example, *enough-cough-bough*, and *meat-great-threat*. However, many of the so-called weird spellings are usually words that are in fairly common use, which gives a person many opportunities to pick up on these peculiarities. Fortunately, about 85 percent of English words have predictable spelling.

The primary aim of all forms of writing is to convey a message to the reader. If writing is regarded as merely a procedure for connecting the auditory and visual patterns of a language, then it should be no great surprise that some of the world's languages lack a written form.

Therefore, when it comes to creating writing experiences, the major goal for parents is to get deaf children excited about writing so that they can put down their ideas on paper. In doing this, they should be given the message that there are two ways to write a word—the right way and the wrong way. Sensible parents know how to strike a balance between nurturing creativity and fostering correct conventions. We agree that the emphasis in early writing should be on fluency rather than on accurate spelling, but this doesn't mean we should throw the baby out with the bath water.

Spelling has to be taught at some point, and because of the irregularities in English, some memorization will be necessary. Spelling instruction, however, should relate to words in the real world, focus on the recognition of patterns, and give children the strategies necessary to correctly spell words that they want to use. We know that today's teachers would never return written assignments, especially in the early grades, with misspellings and grammatical errors heavily marked and corrected in red. Without this kind of intervention, children learn quickly enough that if audiences are going to comprehend their message, then it helps greatly if the spelling is correct. This, in itself, can be a great incentive for them to "get it right."

The arguments made for not being overly concerned about spelling can also be made for punctuation. See the box titled "Is Punctuation Important?" for an example of how punctuation can change the meaning of sentences. Obviously, when a child's written message is unclear, we can expect parents to talk to the child about the intent of the message and to offer kind suggestions about how to make the message understandable by others.

The more writing activities deaf children engage in, the more likely they will come to understand that correctness in spelling and punctuation will help others understand their written message. At this point, we can expect this realization to become a prime motivator in their desire to learn the proper conventions with regards to these two aspects of writing.

Special Opportunities for Deaf Children to Write

Technological advances are making it imperative that deaf children learn to write and read to a greater extent than ever before. Many of these changes affect the way the way deaf people live, because having the ability to make use of these technologies is necessary if they wish to optimize their career and social potential. These technologies include

- Teletype communication (TTY). This is a keyboard that has a built-in coupler that allows a person to type messages over the phone line to someone else who also has a TTY.

Is Punctuation Important?

Dear Johnnie,

I want a man who knows what love is all about. You are generous, kind, and thoughtful. People who are not like you admit to being useless and inferior. You have ruined me for other men. I yearn for you. I have no feelings whatsoever when we are apart. I can be forever happy—will you please let me be yours?

Frankie

Dear John,

I want a man who knows what love is. All about you are generous, kind, and thoughtful people who are not like you. Admit to being useless and inferior! You have ruined me. For other men I yearn. For you, I have no feelings whatsoever. When we are apart, I can be forever happy. Will you please let me be? Yours,

Frances

- Message relay centers (MRC). Message relay centers allow a deaf person to use a TTY to talk to someone who has a phone but not a TTY. An operator at the center is contracted who then dials the phone number required and uses either type or voice to convey the message that the two parties exchange with each other.
- Closed captioning. This enables the captions of TV and video programs to be shown and thus allows printed access to the speech and sounds on the programs.
- Distance education. Classes and workshops are taught via videoconferencing. These classes typically make use of writing on overhead projectors.
- Virtual universities. An increasing number of colleges and universities are offering courses on-line. People who take a course this way need to be able to write because they usually have to submit papers and assignments via their Internet connections; participate

in classroom, on-line, real-time discussions; and respond to their instructor's queries.

- E-mail. E-mail is rapidly becoming society's medium of choice for social interactions outside of personal contact. Even among hearing people, there are significant numbers who prefer e-mail to the phone.
- Internet. One aspect of the Internet can be likened to an extension of the shopping mall. Everything from airfares to cars and homes can be bought on the Internet. To do so, however, a person is required to be able to ask questions, respond to queries, and fill in forms correctly while on-line.
- Alphanumeric pagers. These devices, only slightly bigger than a regular pager, are rapidly gaining in popularity and will soon be as ubiquitous as the cell phone. They allow a person to send and receive phone and e-mail messages by typing on a miniature keyboard.

To this list we can add one firm prediction about the future: More and more print-enabled technologies will be developed, and the necessity for good writing skills will not diminish in the foreseeable future.

Twenty-Five Great Writing Strategies

From our years of interacting with parents with deaf children, we have heard a variety of stories about what they have done to help their children write. We have taken the liberty of sharing some of these with you below.

1. Provide the tools for writing throughout the house. Keep a pile of recycled paper along with pencils, pens, and crayons in different rooms, including the child's bedroom.
2. Keep a white board and washable pen handy to write down what is needed from the store.
3. Write shopping lists together and then group items into categories—meats, vegetables, dairy, and so forth.
4. Introduce your child to children's crosswords and other word games.

5. Plan a birthday party. Make a list of guests and send out invitations. Make place cards for each guest and write out thank-you notes.

6. Arrange for a pen pal. Some schools for deaf children and deaf education programs in public schools have their own Web sites and actively seek pen pals for their students. Be creative and reach out to someone overseas through pen pal Web sites that can be found on the Internet.

7. Have the child write out a plan for a vacation or day trip. Encourage note taking during the trips. These plans and notes do not have to be unduly long and comprehensive. They can be written on any piece of paper or typed up on the computer.

8. Make a family tree. Begin with names and birth dates only, then expand the list to show where everyone now lives; if the child's interest holds, then include places where family members work.

9. Have your child tell you a story, then write it down and read it back. If your child is young enough and enjoys drawing, then have him illustrate the story.

10. Help your child open a bank account, fill out a magazine subscription, or help you complete a free raffle ticket form often found in malls or local papers.

11. Make a book. Use personal photos or pictures from a magazine. Paste these in a book and have him write a word, phrase, or sentence under it. As the child gets older, encourage increasingly more elaborate stories under each picture.

12. Keep a log of daily activities. Logs are simple entries stating what was done with no elaboration. For example,

> Monday, August 13, 2001. Strong winds and rain all day. Stayed inside and looked at old photos. Sloppy Joe's for dinner.

13. Encourage the child to keep a diary. This is a simple-sounding activity but is rather difficult even for adults to do. Keep your expectations reasonable. An occasional entry is far better than arguing for daily entries.

14. Write the occasional directives and encourage the child to do the same thing. You might write, "Please turn the oven on to 375

degrees and walk the dog," whereas your child might write, "Take me to a movie. Make me pizza for dinner, please."

15. Have a family message board where the family can leave messages and notes for each other, such as where they are going, what they are doing, and what time they will be home.

16. Write a letter to someone together.

17. Have the child watch you write out checks or use the Internet to pay bills. At some point, see if he can guide you through the entire process—either by writing out the check and mailing it or by going through each step of the on-line banking process.

18. Create do-it-yourself books, such as *My Wish Book, My Secret Book,* and *My Book about Me.*

19. Patchwork letters. Cut out letters from a magazine or newspaper and paste them together to make words. Later, create sentences from the words. See who can create the funniest sentence from a group of words.

20. For older children whose reading skills are advanced enough to read the newspaper, try proofreading the local newspaper for typographical errors.

21. Use a local map to work out the best route to a certain destination. Have your child write the directions down for getting from your home to another place and back again.

22. Make a list of videos and rank them using a five-star ranking system or simple statements, such as "I loved this one and want to watch it again."

23. If going on a vacation or a trip, have your child make a list of things they want to take and things they want to do while on the trip This is an activity that everyone usually enjoys doing no matter how old they are.

24. Write a paragraph to include in the family Christmas letter.

25. Write out the clues for a game of "Treasure Hunt" around the house.

Now, you get started on your way to making writing a habit around the house by adding five more great strategies for encouraging your deaf child to write.

Conclusion

A parent's role in promoting an enjoyment for writing in their deaf child is one that centers around the provision of activities that encourage writing. This is likely to occur when parents do the following:

- Provide the tools for writing (crayons, pens, paper, computer).
- Model writing behaviors around the house.
- Show that writing has many useful functions in our daily lives.
- Provide opportunities for the child to write at home.
- Encourage family efforts to write.

Even children who desire to write are often faced with the formidable task of overcoming the appeal of television, computer games, and the Internet. Every parent with children, deaf and hearing, struggles with ways to lessen the effects of these distractions. While we acknowledge that these ubiquitous household activities carry some modicum of intellectual value, they cut drastically into the amount of time that a child has available for writing at home—time that is further reduced by other after-school activities, such as playing sports, completing household chores, doing homework, and playing with friends. There are no easy solutions; but just as deaf children try hard in their effort to learn to read and write, you too, need to be persistent in your effort to support them.

CHAPTER 9

Working with Schools

This chapter will help you understand

- How parents can be active participants in the education of their deaf child
- How parents and teachers can help each other
- Strategies for getting along with teachers and other school personnel

---

Parents are their children's best advocates at home, at school, and in the community. And that's the way it should be, given that almost every research finding since the Coleman et al. seminal study in 1966 has shown that of all the variables that impacted on student academic performance, the most significant was home environment. A similar finding has been found for deaf children (Moores 2001). Parental involvement in schools is highly related not only to a student's academic achievement but also to his improved behavior (fewer discipline problems), better attendance at school, and greater self-esteem. Because of these results, most teachers are aware of the importance of connecting with their students' parents, and generally, they regard parents as valued and empowered team members in the educational process.

The evidence supporting parental involvement in schools has led to a marked change in the nature of this participation. In the not too distant past, parents were expected to drop their child off at the school gate and let the teacher get on with the task of teaching him. When parents were asked to participate, the expectation was for simple clerical chores, such as running off worksheets, or for fundraising efforts, such as bake sales and raffles to buy computers or library books. The one educational effort required of everyone was the hallowed task of signing and returning the student's report card.

Today, parental involvement means much more than this, and in the education of deaf children, parents are expected to carry out the following:

- Seek out professional support services at the time of diagnosis of their child's hearing loss.
- Adopt a communication system that is compatible with family values and the deaf child's educational and social needs.
- Attend all Individual Family Service Plan (IFSP) meetings for their child when he is an infant or preschooler.
- Attend all Individual Educational Plan (IEP) meetings for their school-age child.
- Be aware of their rights as parents and their child's right to educational services as mandated by the Individuals with Disabilities Educational Act (IDEA).
- Provide a home environment that allows their child to do homework without undue distractions.
- Purchase or obtain technologies that help to access communication. These include TTYs, closed-captioned televisions, hearing aids, sound alerting devices, and more.
- Monitor their child's homework and offer help as needed.
- Engage their child in educational activities at home and in the community.
- Attend displays and performances in which their child is involved at school.
- Volunteer in classrooms when work schedule permits.
- Participate in fundraising and other development activities sponsored by the school.
- Participate in parent-support groups with other families of deaf children. (The American Society for Deaf Children is a national organization that hosts an excellent Web site, http://www.deafchildren.org, that offers ideas and resources that will help

parents support one another and promote their deaf child's education and well-being.)

It can be argued that all parents have to face up to many of these responsibilities, but the pressure on hearing parents of deaf children may be greater because of the additional challenge of having to modify their own way of life so that it becomes more compatible with that of their deaf child. This challenge stems from the deaf child's dependency on his field of vision for communicating and may necessitate changes in how the hearing parents communicate with their child and how they arrange their homes to be visually accessible for him.

Although it might be that all parents have their child's best interests at heart, it is also true that not all parents know how to advocate on behalf of their child's education. One might surmise that parents who are professionals with extensive education beyond their high school years will, by virtue of these educational experiences and through contacts with many other people, turn out to be the best advocates. Similarly, parents who do not have any time to spend at the school with their child and who show no interest in connecting with his teachers will greatly disadvantage his chances for educational success. To some extent, both of these suppositions are correct.

Yet, some of the best advocates whom we have met have themselves had little education and belonged to a low-income bracket. One such mother of two deaf children had this to say about her way of bringing up her children and her involvement with their school:

> When my children were in elementary school, I went to all the PTA meetings. I helped in the school kitchen when I wasn't working. When they were in high school, I never attended any school things even though I lived one block away from the school. I was too busy raising them and my other two children at home where I worked as a homemaker. I spent a lot of time with my children. I went with them everywhere, but I didn't interfere with what their teachers were doing. What could I do, I never even finished school?

Both of her deaf children went on to university, with one receiving a doctorate and the other a bachelor's degree. Her unwitting approach to advocacy was to be there for her children and to put her complete trust in the school. This is not the right approach for all parents, but for this mother, it worked out well.

On the other hand, some of the poorest advocates that we have encountered were parents who were teachers, social workers, or successful business people. These parents acted as if their status as a professional gave them a license to oversee and tell their deaf child's teachers what instructional methods they should be using in the classroom. They were vigilant in their tracking of their child's schooling, yet what they succeeded in doing was to infuse their parent–teacher relationship with feelings of alienation, distrust, and resentment. The teachers reacted by not wanting the children of these parents in their classroom for the following year. Oftentimes, a poor parent–teacher situation can adversely affect the children to such a degree that they will not reach their academic potential and will exhibit behaviors that are detrimental not only to their own learning but also to that of their classmates.

Good advocacy is not genetically endowed. All parents have the potential to do what is in the best interest for their child. The focus of this chapter is to help you become an effective advocate for your deaf child's education by looking at how you can work with schools to help your child's literacy skills grow.

Challenges to Parent Participation

There are a variety of reasons why parents might feel apprehensive about making contact with teachers. Some of these reasons are cultural in nature. For example, with some ethnic minority groups, there exists a belief that a parent's role in education starts and ends in the home (Grossman 1995). These parents do not approach school authorities for help because they see their own ethnic community as being the place to handle any concerns that they might have about their child's education. Other groups, and especially immigrants, might feel intimidated by authority figures, and for that reason, they avoid contact with the school.

Other reasons for the apprehension of parents in dealing with school personnel are more general and include a lack of knowledge concerning school matters, a reluctance to confront experts with their own ideas about education, and occasionally unpleasant memories of their own experiences at school. There is also a bevy of more mundane obstacles to parent participation that include work schedules, difficulty finding transport to the school, inadequate child-care resources, and other pressing responsibilities related to the needs of other family members. All of these reasons are important to the family.

On the obverse side of the coin, there are some teachers who may inadvertently hinder parent–teacher relationships by giving parents a very limited role in their child's education and by ignoring their opinions. Whatever the reasons might be for a lack of a strong parent–teacher relationship, the fact remains that the stronger the relationship, the better the opportunity children will have for learning.

A Strong Parent–Teacher Relationship

Research has looked into ways to affect a better bridge between schools and parents, and there is no shortage of ideas. Many of these ideas are common sense, and what they require most from parents is a commitment to follow through on them. For example, Epstein (1995) identified the following six types of two-way cooperation between families and schools:

1. Parenting. Families provide for the health and safety of their children and maintain an environment conducive to learning and good behavior; and schools provide information for the parents on child development and ways to support changes that the child will experience.
2. Communicating. Families inform the schools of their concerns and their needs, and the schools provide the families with information about school programs and student progress (which will include the time-honored and ubiquitous methods, such as

report cards, parent conferences, phone calls, and parent meetings). New information goes home in a written form that is hopefully not so voluminous that it gets the same treatment as junk
mail.

3. Volunteering. Parents can make significant contributions to the
   functioning of the school, and the school can get the best out of volunteers by matching the interest, talent, and expertise of parents
   with the needs of the various classrooms.
4. Home learning. Family members supervise and assist their child
   at home with school assignments, and the teachers provide the
   necessary guidance and support for these tasks.
5. Decision making. Parents take meaningful roles in the school
   decision-making process, and schools open up this opportunity
   to as many parents as possible.
6. Collaborating. Families help the school participate in community
   events (e.g., food banks, recycling), and schools help families access support services (e.g., child care, health care, and cultural
   and social events).

Inside school, the teacher should be your child's strongest advocate. This might sound like a trite statement, but the teacher's
ability to support your child's education is dependent upon many
factors, including their relationship with you. This is why textbooks
for teachers often devote considerable space to talking about how
teachers can foster a strong parent–teacher relationship. Stewart
and Kluwin (2001), for instance, in their book titled, *Teaching Deaf
and Hard of Hearing Students,* offered the following six principles for
teachers wishing to connect with parents:

1. Be a good listener.
2. Ask parents for advice about the best way for you [the teacher] to
   communicate school matters to them.
3. Present your opinions without intimidation.
4. Respond promptly and courteously to a parent's question or
   request for information.
5. Show your positive side.
6. Be a good resource person.

But a relationship is a two-way street, and unless a parent is willing to contribute in a positive manner to the work at the school, neither the teacher nor the parent will be an effective advocate. The following five principles can help you get along with your child's teachers:

1. Be an Informed Parent

Your child's teachers are valuable resource people; therefore, use them to help you find information. Schools do not expect parents to become an expert in all matters pertaining to the education of deaf children. But what you do know about the education of your own child can be of tremendous help to the school. The road to being an informed parent starts at the time of diagnosis, when parents will soon have to make decisions regarding the type of language and the communication method that they are going to use with their child. Once you have learned about the options available, it is again your responsibility to get as much information about each option as you can so that you can make further informed decisions. School personnel can direct you to people who can share with you their feelings about the choices that they have made, but do not expect or permit teachers and others to make decisions for you. This remains your responsibility.

As your child progresses through the school years, you will find it helpful to know something about the different instructional methods being used, such as individual versus group teaching and structured approaches to learning language versus holistic approaches. Knowing about these and other educational strategies will make it easier for teachers and other school personnel to talk with you about their ideas for teaching your child. It will also help you to know what kind of questions to ask at IEP and parent–teacher meetings. (See the Web site of the Laurent Clerc National Deaf Education Center, http:// clerccenter.gallaudet.edu, for a comprehensive list of current teaching ideas and issues relating to the education of deaf children.)

2. Respond to the Teacher's Request for Information and Help

This is a convenient way to demonstrate your interest in your child's education. Teachers normally send out requests because they are looking for information or materials that will help them in the classroom. The following are examples of requests that teachers might make:

- Permission for your child to go on a field trip
- Your availability to join a field trip
- Your help as a classroom parent with responsibilities for organizing events or helping with a fundraising activity
- Your willingness to read books to the class, do an art project, or perform some other school activity on a monthly basis
- Supplies for a science experiment or an art project
- Signing a form that verifies your child has read for a certain period of time
- Providing information about your family to build a family tree

3. Attend and Be Prepared for All Parent–Teacher Meetings

This is an absolute must for parents. Get the agenda before the date of the IEP meeting. Look over the items that are going to be discussed, and ask the teacher which of the items should be highlighted for particular attention. If there is anything on the agenda with which you are unfamiliar, contact the teacher or the person responsible for running the IEP and ask for clarification. If you have a specific concern, then have it added to the IEP agenda prior to the meeting so that the other participants can have an opportunity to think about the concern and prepare a response to it. The better prepared everyone is at the IEP, the better chance that a program will be developed that is appropriate for your child.

Signing an IEP form is only the beginning of your responsibility for your child's education. The parent–teacher conferences that often follow each report card are good opportunities for you to keep abreast of mid-semester or mid-year academic and social progress. They provide you and the teacher with a chance to share success stories about what your child has achieved inside and outside of school. Both parties also have the opportunity to raise any concerns they may have about what the child is doing or not doing. Too often, parents are simply content if their child passes the year and moves on to the next grade, so they wait until the end of the semester, or even the end of the school year, to find out about their child's accomplishments. Passing is not enough. More important than an A or B or C on the report card is the interest and effort that your child is showing toward each school subject, and this should be discussed at all meetings.

4. Be Open to How Teachers Teach

Some of the characteristics that apply to good teaching include creativity, consistency in providing positive reinforcement, commitment to providing prompt feedback on assignments, respect, and good work ethics. Good teachers also bring to the classroom their own bag of idiosyncrasies relating to teaching. These personal traits allow them to make adjustments to their teaching in order to accommodate the diverse learning styles of their students. Therefore, among several teachers there might be a variety of different instructional approaches for helping a student meet his academic goals, and each of these approaches will reflect that particular teacher's personal teaching style.

5. Ask the Teacher What You Can Do

Behind every student who succeeds in the classroom is a good parent. Teachers know very well that children who have parents who work with them at home are more likely to do better in school than those who do not have supportive parents. Therefore, if you are uncertain about what you can do with your child at home, ask the teacher for advice. The following are some questions that we have heard parents ask:

• What magazines would be good to subscribe to for my child?
• What math words can I use around the house to reinforce concepts he is learning at school?
• We are going to the town's museum. What are some things that I can talk about with my child before, during, and after the trip?
• How much help would you like me to give my child while he is doing his science homework?

- What educational Web sites can you suggest that I explore with my child?
- I noticed that my child's grade has slipped in writing. Is there anything that I can do at home to help him improve his writing skills?

In sum, your goal in a parent–teacher relationship is to be a parent with whom a teacher feels comfortable sharing information about your child's educational progress. You are not aiming to be the teacher's friend nor do you want twenty-four-hour access to the teacher by phone, e-mail, or in person during school hours (and neither will the teacher!). What you do want, however, is for the teacher to respect your requests for information or help and to respond appropriately and promptly. Finally, be positive in your interactions with teachers and other school personnel, and you will find that they will respond to you in like fashion.

Working with Schools to Achieve Literacy Goals

Although we have stated the importance of parental involvement many times throughout this book, we cannot overemphasize that such positive parental involvement will influence their children's school achievement. In the area of literacy development, at the very least, parental involvement will likely yield the following results:

- An increase in the occurrence of the child's literacy and literacy-related experiences
- A strong message sent to the child about the importance of school
- An affirmation reaches the teacher that the parents care about their child's schooling (Sonneschein and Schmidt 2000)

If you accept that there are benefits, the question then becomes: What can you do with teachers and other school personnel that will facilitate your child's acquisition of literacy skills? The ideas offered in the previous sections will help parental involvement in general terms, but with respect to literacy development, the following suggestions could help.

Understand the Literacy Goals in Your Child's IEP

Understand the literacy goals and objectives that have been written in your child's IEP. Literacy goals in an IEP are usually stated in terms of reading and writing skills and are generally broad and oriented to long-term accomplishments. Examples of such goals are as follows:

> Jonn will improve his reading skills one grade level in one school year.

IEP objectives, on the other hand, are more specific and provide some idea about how the long-term goals will be achieved. Examples of objectives that are related to the goal just described are

> Jonn will complete the Scholastic's second-grade reading program.

> He will read one extra book with a second-grade reading level every month. This book will be read at school and at home.

> He will write four short storybooks in class that will each contain twenty new vocabulary words. Upon completion, these books will be read aloud at home.

When you attend an IEP meeting, feel comfortable asking about the reading and writing goals and objectives. Make sure that they are stated in terms that you understand and that they represent reasonable levels of achievement and work for your child. (For more ideas about IEPs, see Stewart and Luetke-Stahlman 1998.)

Understand Your Child's Current Reading and Writing Levels

The average deaf child lags behind same-age hearing peers in his development of reading and writing skills. Ask your child's teacher what your child's reading level is and what the implications are at this level for learning social studies, science, math, and language arts. Inquire about your child's ability to understand assigned reading materials and what accommodations will be made in the event that the reading level of the materials is too high. Ask also about your child's ability to write responses to questions. You do not want your child's knowledge of a subject matter to be penalized because he is presently unable to properly write a response. There are alternative ways for getting a response from a child that include responding verbally to questions, selecting the correct answer in a multiple-choice question, or demonstrating his comprehension of a concept through a hands-on activity. Another way to learn about your child's reading and writing levels is to exchange letters with him or to help him write letters to other people—a strategy that helped one long-time teacher of deaf children learn to write when she was a child (see box titled "Resurrect the Practice of Writing Letters").

Understand Your Classroom's Literacy Program

In the classroom, it is the teacher's responsibility to translate IEP goals and objectives into instructional programs that run the gamut from total dependency on textbook-generated lessons to prepared lesson plans. Find out how the teacher plans to meet the IEP goals and objectives. Ask her to show you the literacy materials being used, the expected time lines for completion of certain reading and writing activities, and the assessment tools that will be used to monitor progress.

Share Your Ideas about Reading and Writing with the Teacher

Your culture and the values and beliefs that you hold will have helped shape your thoughts about reading and writing in school. Teachers can benefit from knowing how you feel about what they are doing, what types of books you read at home, the types of books that you would like to see your child read, the opportunities you have at home for exploring literacy, and constraints that might adversely affect your child's learning, such as having no adult supervision in the evening. Read the box titled "What Happens at Home Matters," to hear about Andrea's description of how her parents helped her learn to read. Now think about what you do at home to support reading. Delpit (1986) provided a good illustration of how her understanding of what the parents wanted in her reading pro-

Resurrect the Practice of Writing Letters

Do you remember when your parents used to handwrite letters to friends, send extended notes in Christmas cards, and shared with you letters that they have received from relatives? The practice of writing a letter and mailing it to a friend is being supplanted by e-mails and inexpensive long-distance calling. But as we struggle to keep up with the myriad of opportunities for communicating that computer technology has provided us, we should pause to reflect on the value inherent in writing a letter with pen and paper. Maureen is a deaf woman who has taught English at a school for deaf children for over thirty years. She also attended a school for deaf children as a child at a time when children remained in the dormitory all through the year except for a couple of weeks over the Christmas holidays and two months off during the summer. Maureen's parents encouraged her to write letters to her schoolmates as a way of keeping in touch. Her father would read the drafts of each letter and correct mistakes in grammar and vocabulary. Maureen would then read the corrections, rewrite the letter, and mail it off. Consider this father–daughter literacy connection for a moment. If you are an avid user of e-mails, recall the last time you shared an e-mail message with your deaf child? Similarly, when was the last time you read an e-mail message that your deaf child had written? We acknowledge that a person's privacy should be respected, but at some point, a child can be introduced to the intimacy of the letters that his parents write, and parents should be available to help him develop an ease for writing letters to others. This is but one manner in which parents can support their child's journey to becoming literate.

gram influenced the instructional method she used in the classroom. Her experiences are also described by Sonnenschein and Schmidt (2000) in the following:

She began by utilizing practices that emphasized the use of authentic literature as a tool for instruction. Her approach was consistent with recommendations from theorists and researchers. However, Delpit's

What Happens at Home Matters

Talking to deaf adults who are good readers reveals a myriad of activities that they have done at home that helped them hone their reading skills. Following is one story that Andrea, a deaf adult, told us:

One of the factors that strongly influenced my ability to learn to read was my early exposure to books and bookstores. When we spent time in England, my dad took me to second-hand bookshops where I could select one book—any book—as long as it didn't cost an arm and a leg. I felt awfully grown up being charged with the responsibility of selecting a book for myself, which was why I took hours to make my selection; but when it was done, I treasured that book even if the reading level was beyond me. Later, I bought new books, such as the Bobbsey Twins series. These are not what would be categorized as great literature, but their adventures gave me great enjoyment and whetted my imagination and desire to read more. I also was allowed to buy comics and the wonderful Classics Illustrated series, which paved the way for my reading the original unabridged novels later.

At home, I remember my mom poring over cookbooks before a dinner party. She would tell me what she was going to make and even invited me to prepare a dish or two with her. Of course, she gave me some recipes to read. My parents read a lot too for their own enjoyment, and although I cannot remember them ever reading aloud to me, I do recall pestering them about their reading material and asking them to share with me their opinions of the books they were reading and the reasons why they liked them. I still remember their favorite writers, some of whom became my own.

My parents also wrote quite a bit. I was very proud when made privy to Mom's letters to her friends, parents, and siblings when we lived abroad. I was also shown the replies and got a charge out of them. I learned from my mother and father that one cannot read without reflecting, which, when you think about it, would be like eating without digesting.

African American students did not progress and their parents were critical of her approach. The parents wanted Delpit to use a more traditional approach that emphasized fundamental skills. When Delpit changed her approach to a more traditional one, the children progressed. (269)

Keep in mind that you are not being asked to dictate how you think a teacher should teach. The ideas you share are valuable because they may lead the teacher to instructional approaches that are more compatible with your child's cultural background and style of learning.

Ask for Specific Directions to Help at Home with Reading and Writing

Teachers must understand that simply telling parents what they can do might not sufficiently spur them on to greater involvement nor is it good enough for a teacher to just send books home. Ask the teacher for specific ideas so that you can match activities with one or more of the literacy goals she has for your child. For example, if the teacher sends a book home for your child to read, depending upon the age of your child, you might want to ask one or more of the following questions:

- Are there any particular vocabulary words that I should be pointing out and discussing with my child?
- Should I read aloud parts of the book?
- Should my child read aloud parts of the book? What do I do if he doesn't like to read aloud?
- About how much time everyday should my child spend reading this book?
- If my child can't answer questions assigned to the story, can I help him find the answer in the book? How do I do this? Do I point to the answer? Should I have him read the page that the answer is on? Do I ask other questions that might lead to the answer?
- If I don't know the signs for some of the words in the book, what should I do when I am reading aloud?
- Should I have him write two or three sentences that describe what each chapter is about?

Remember, teachers care that you care. Do not be shy about asking for directions about what you can do at home.

Parent–Teacher Conferences

These meetings should be informative, but they can also be a cause of dissatisfaction. A child can be bothered when parents and teachers discuss him behind his back. Parents may also be somewhat embarrassed about sitting on small chairs listening to reports on their child's classroom performance and general behavior. Teachers themselves (especially the less experienced) may also feel ill at ease when telling either an apprehensive or an aggressive parent about her child's problems. Because of these uncomfortable but not uncommon scenarios, it is important that teachers and parents attempt to create and develop a rapport with each other that encourages open communication between them right from the very beginning. The teacher should let the parents know when and how she can be contacted, make every effort to include them in meetings and other activities, and show that she sincerely values their input. A teacher who makes the effort and takes the time to listen to parents will soon get to know their goals, interests, and concerns and, hence, be in a very good position to give advice on a continuing basis rather than just at the biannual parent–teacher conference.

Good teachers welcome an ongoing dialogue with parents because it gives them a much better understanding of their students. Parents also have the right to expect from the teacher periodic updates on their child's progress and timely notification of any problems he may be having. In the parent–teacher relationship, communication is the key. Frequent communication between teacher and parent will ensure a conference meeting where an atmosphere of trust prevails, where unexpected issues seldom arise, and where specific information can now help to reinforce or modify the teacher's previous suggestions for how the parents could help at home to support what is being done in the particular educational program that their child attends.

Get the Word Out: You're a Volunteer!

Family volunteers in schools engage in a variety of endeavors; sometimes in supervision (field trips, yard activities, etc.) and at other times in tasks more directly related to academics, such as reading stories or giving individual help in computer classes. Meeting and working with the teachers is an excellent way to show that you are concerned about your child's education and that you want to be involved. One major benefit of volunteering in the classroom is that by observing the teachers interacting with your child, you can learn firsthand whether the targets set and the methods being used match with your own expectations and goals concerning the "whats" and "hows" of your child's education.

Volunteer time, will of course, be an individual matter because it will hinge on other commitments. Single parents who have to juggle the demands of work and parenting with volunteering will need a lot more flexibility than other parents who can free themselves on a regular basis. Parents may have more than one job, work in the evening, and have other children at home who need their attention. These and many other such responsibilities can prevent them from committing time to volunteer at school. The solution to this equation is a personal matter, and often it is not easy.

It is good protocol for you to aim at helping the whole class or group of students rather than just your own child. As well as keeping within the limits of the teacher's requirements, you should develop a strong respect for the individuality of each student so that you become more responsive to their particular needs. But caution is also required because sometimes a volunteer will inadvertently overstep her position and move into a teaching role. This occurs because it is easy for the volunteer to get emotionally involved in how a student might approach a problem or find a solution. Nevertheless, such involvement might be counterproductive to the child's education if the teacher does not agree with the parent's direction or explanation. Generally, considerate communication between the teacher and parent will provide an adequate schema of what a parent should and should not do in a classroom. As long as the volunteer's duties are clearly specified (as they generally are), unfavorable classroom situations involving the volunteer are likely to occur only on rare occasions.

Another potentially troublesome occasion arises when fiscal cutbacks lead to a reduction of ancillary staff, and the parents find themselves doing replacement work. This happens because the workload will greatly increase after the cuts are made. Administrators, however, are generally sensitive to this situation and make the necessary arrangements to avoid possible conflict and tension from developing between volunteers and those in paid positions.

In the final analysis, schools do realize that parents have a range of skills and talents that make them quite effective as volunteers and that these assets should not be ignored. We encourage all parents to build a strong rapport with faculty at the school and, whenever possible, to become a volunteer.

It will also help if you would provide the school with enough biographical information for the administration to be aware of your skills and aspirations so that you can be placed in the most appropriate situation. In return for your help, you will obtain a firsthand understanding of how the school or educational setting works as well as the teachers' views on the communication systems and types of programs available. These data are valuable because they can help you resolve some of your most difficult problems, such as choosing the best method of communication and the most appropriate type of educational setting for your child.

Conclusion

Parents are their children's best advocates for learning at home and at school. It has been shown that parent involvement in school activities is significantly related to better academic performance, behavior, attendance, and self-esteem. There are many aspects of parental involvement, and they include parenting, communicating, volunteering, home learning, decision-making, and collaborating. It is most important for parents to be aware of the progress that their deaf child is making in school, and this will occur when there is frequent communication between teacher and parent that focuses on the educational needs of the child. Frequent contact should also ensure that the parent–teacher conference contains no surprises but rather will emphasize what the school is doing for the student and reinforce how the parents can help at home to support the particular literacy program that the school has developed for their deaf child.

BIBLIOGRAPHY

Bailes, C. N. 2001. Integrative ASL-English language arts: Bridging paths to literacy. *Sign Language Studies* 1 (2): 147–74.

Berrigan, D., and S. Berrigan. 2000. Bridget and books: Fingerspelling, reading—and sleeping—with print. *Odyssey* 1 (3): 6–9.

Blamey, P., and E. M. Clark. 1985. A wearable multi-electrode speech processor for the profoundly deaf. *Journal of the Acoustical Society of America* 77:1619–21.

Blumenthal-Kelly, A. 1995. Fingerspelling interaction: A set of deaf parents and their deaf daughter. In *Sociolinguistics in Deaf communities,* ed. C. Lucas, 62–73. Washington, D.C.: Gallaudet University Press.

Bornstein, H., K. L. Saulnier, and L. B. Hamilton, eds. 1983. *The comprehensive Signed English dictionary.* Washington, D.C.: Kendall Green.

Brady, S., and D. Shankweiler, eds. 1996. *Phonological processes in literacy.* Hillsdale, N.J.: Lawrence Erlbaum.

Bransford, J., ed. 2000. *How people learn.* Washington, D.C.: National Academy Press.

Clarke, B. R. 1983. Competence in communication for hearing impaired children. *B.C. Journal of Special Education* 1:15–28.

Cochlear Corporation. 1998. Issues and answers: The Nucleus Cochlear Implant system. Englewood, Colo.: Cochlear Corporation. Booklet.

Coleman, J. S., E. Q. Campbell, C. J. Hobson, J. McPartland, A. M. Mood, F. D. Weinfeld, and R. L. York. 1966. *Equality of educational opportunity.* Washington, D.C.: U.S. Government Printing Office.

Cornett, R. O. 1967. Cued Speech. *American Annals of the Deaf* 112: 3–13.

Curtiss, S. 1989. The independence and task specificity of language. In *Interaction in human development,* ed. A. Bornstein and J. Bruner. Hillsdale, N.J.: Lawrence Erlbaum.

Davis, J. 1944. *Mother tongue.* New York: Carol.

Delpit, L. D. 1986. Skills and other dilemmas of a progressive black educator. *Harvard Educational Review* 56:379–85.

Dillon, H. 2001. *Hearing aids.* New York: Thieme.

Doman, G. 1975. *How to teach your baby to read.* New York: Doubleday.

Duhatschek, E. 2001. Striking well before the deadline. *The Globe and Mail,* 10 March.

Epstein, J. L. 1995. School-family-community partnership: Caring for children we share. *Phi Delta Kappan* 76 (9): 701–12.

Erber, N. P. 1972. Auditory visual recognition of speech. *Journal of Speech and Hearing Research* 15:413–22.

Flesch, R. 1955. *Why Johnny can't read.* New York: Harper.

Garretson, M. D. 1995. Developing communication in the family. In *Kid-friendly parenting with deaf and hard of hearing children,* ed. D. Medwid and D. C. Weston, 70–72. Washington, D.C.: Clerc.

Gelb, M. J. 1998. *How to think like Leonardo da Vinci: Seven steps to genius every day.* New York: Delacorte.

Grant, J. 1967. *The hearing impaired: Birth to six.* San Diego: College Hill.

Grossman, H. 1995. *Special education in a diverse society.* Boston: Allyn and Bacon.

Gustason, G., D. Pfetzing, and E. Zawolkow. 1980. *Signing Exact English.* Los Alamitos, Calif.: Modern Signs.

Heidinger, V. A. 1984. *Analyzing syntax and semantics.* Washington, D.C.: Gallaudet College Press.

Kjelgaard, J. 1945. *Big Red.* New York: Scholastic.

Lang, H. G. 2000. *A phone of our own: The Deaf insurrection against Ma Bell.* Washington, D.C.: Gallaudet University Press.

Luetke-Stahlman, B. 1996. *One mother's story: An educator becomes a parent.* Los Alamitos, Calif.: Modern Signs.

Luetke-Stahlman, B. 1998. *Language issues in deaf education.* Hillsboro, Oreg.: Butte Publications.

McAnally, P. L., S. Rose, and S. P. Quigley. 1998. *Language learning practices with deaf children.* 2d. ed. Austin: Pro-Ed.

Moores, D. F. 2001. *Educating the deaf: Psychology, principles, and practices.* 5th ed. Boston: Houghton-Mifflin.

Muma, J., and H. Teller. 2001. Developments in cognitive socialization: Implications for deaf education. *American Annals of the Deaf* 146:31–38.

Musselman, C. 2000. How do children who can't hear learn to read an alphabetic script? A review of the literature on reading and deafness. *Journal of Deaf Studies and Deaf Education* 5 (1):9–31.

National Center for Educational Statistics. 1998. Literacy in OECD countries. *Technical report on the first international adult literacy survey.* Washington, D.C.: U.S. Department of Education.

Neeley, B. M. 2000. Calling up literacy. *Odyssey* 1 (3):22–25.

Nelson, K. 1966. *Language in cognitive development*. New York: Cambridge University Press.

Owens, R. 1988. *Language development*. Columbus, Ohio: Merrill.

Paul, P. 1998. *Literacy and deafness: The development of reading, writing, and literate thought*. Boston: Allyn and Bacon.

Pinker, S. 1984. *Language learnability and language development*. Cambridge, Mass.: Harvard University Press.

_____. 1994. *The language instinct*. New York: William Morrow.

Pintner, R., and D. G. Paterson. 1917. *A scale of performance tests*. New York: Appelton.

Ree, J. 1999. *I see a voice*. London: HarperCollins.

Roberts, P. 1967. *Modern grammar*. New York: Brace and World.

Rymer, R. 1993. *Genie: An abused child's flight from silence*. New York: HarperCollins.

Schaller, S. 1991. *A man without words*. New York: Summit.

Schein, J. D., and D. A. Stewart. 1995. *Language in motion: Exploring the nature of sign*. Washington, D.C.: Gallaudet University Press.

Schleper, D. 2000. Fingerspelling—for literacy. *Odyssey* 1 (3):10.

Seuss, Dr. 1960. *Green eggs and ham*. New York: Random House.

_____. 1974. *There's a wocket in my pocket!* New York: Random House.

Singleton, J., and E. Newport. 1993. The acquisition of sign language from impoverished input. *Cognitive Science* 14:11–28.

Sonnenschein, S., and D. Schmidt. 2000. Fostering home and community connections to support children's reading. In *Engaging young readers*, ed. L. Baker, M. J. Dreher, and J. T. Guthrie, 264–84. New York: Guildford.

Spencer, P. 2001. A good start: Suggestions for visual communications with deaf and hard of hearing babies and toddlers. Available at http://clerccenter2.gallaudet.edu/KidsWorldDeafNet/e-docs/visual-conversations.

Stewart, D. A. 1998. *American Sign Language the easy way*. Hauppauge, N.Y.: Barron's Educational.

Stewart, D. A., and T. N. Kluwin. 2001. *Teaching deaf and hard of hearing students: Content, strategies, and curriculum*. Boston: Allyn and Bacon.

Stewart, D. A., and B. Luetke-Stahlman. 1998. *The signing family: What every parent should know about sign communication*. Washington, D.C.: Clerc.

Stinson, K. 1982. *Red Is best*. Toronto: Annick.

Stokoe, W. C. 1978. Sign language versus spoken language. *Sign Language Studies* 18:69–90.

Stubbs, M. 1983. *Discourse analysis: The sociolinguistic analysis of natural language.* Chicago: University of Chicago Press.

Stynes, B. W. 1997. *Walking with Mama.* Nevada City, Calif.: Dawn.

Tartter, V. C. 1986. *Language processes.* New York: Holt, Rinehart and Winston.

Venturini, D. 2000. A family embraces books with a daughter. *Odyssey* 1 (3):34–39.

Ward, S. 2000. *Baby talk.* London: Century.

Wilbur, R. 2000. The use of ASL to support the development of English and literacy. *Journal of Deaf Studies and Deaf Education* 5 (1):81–104.

Yurkowski, P., and C. Ewolt. 1986. A case for the semantic processing of the deaf reader. *American Annals of the Deaf* 131: 243–47.

INDEX

ABOUT THE AUTHORS

David Stewart is Professor in the Deaf Education Program at Michigan State University. Following in the steps of his mentor Dr. Clarke, he began his career teaching deaf children and has worked with families of deaf children for over two decades. He is a prolific writer and has published books on a range of topics that reflect his journey through life as a deaf professional, teacher, researcher, and sports enthusiast. Book topics include American Sign Language, teaching methodologies, sign communication for families, Deaf sports, and interpreting. He was awarded the David Peikoff Chair of Deafness Studies and has made numerous national and international presentations. He believes in nurturing the strengths of every child so that their dreams can blossom forth.

Bryan Clarke is Professor Emeritus at the University of British Columbia in Vancouver, Canada. He has worked with deaf children and their parents since 1955 and has prepared teachers of deaf students in both Australia, his native land, and Canada, where he has spent the past thirty years. He has won several prestigious awards for his teaching and research. He has long proposed that the classroom teaching of reading be merged with the realities of deaf children's everyday lives at home and in the community. He wistfully notes that there is a wide gulf between the perceptions of children and their teachers (and parents) and suggests that the least we can do is to try to narrow the gap.